Flourishing Enterprise

"A much needed business manifesto that shifts the focus of corporate sustainability to the pursuit of profit opportunities aimed at solving global challenges instead of only doing less harm. Through practices that reconnect us to what we care deeply about, it proposes to harness creativity and collaboration in service of a more prosperous and flourishing world."

—L. HUNTER LOVINS, President, Natural Capitalism Solutions and co-author of *Natural Capitalism*

"The genius of this book lies in its marriage of inspiration with investigation, poetry with practice, and resilience with research. Its long view sets it apart from other books on the topic, and takes the conversation about business, sustainability, and spirituality from the margins into the mainstream."

—MARGARET BENEFIEL, author of *Soul at Work* and *The Soul of a Leader*

"In a business world where growth and profit is king, *Flourishing Enterprise* provides an inspiring alternative to what success can look like and how to achieve it. I highly recommend it for business leaders and managers at all organizational levels."

—DAVID BAKER, Senior Manager, The Boeing Company

"*Flourishing Enterprise* boldly shifts the focus of sustainability. Taking a long view of institutional transformation, it foresees a world in which businesses thrive in service of a prosperous world, contributing positively to a path where all life can flourish on the earth forever. An inspirational guide to the business community for doing well by doing good."

—REBECCA CHOPP, President, Swarthmore College

"What I like most about this book is that it provokes us to think bigger. There is a lot of progress in this direction—a lot of necessary progress. It's at the front edge of the evolving science of leadership."
—RICH LYONS, Dean, Haas School of Business, UC Berkeley

"*Flourishing Enterprise* is one of the most important books of the 21st century. It elucidates what we all long for: genuine happiness and how to align our spirituality and our vocation—our life's work. It offers the possibility for co-creating flourishing communities and enterprises of genuine well-being."
—MARK ANIELSKI, author of *The Economics of Happiness*

"*Flourishing Enterprise* is both deeply insightful and hugely practical for those of us engaged in the future of industry. It is a compelling, inspirational, and passionate guide that takes us into the heart of a new paradigm where life-enhancing business becomes reality."
—GILES HUTCHINS, author of *The Illusion of Separation* and *The Nature of Business*

"*Flourishing Enterprise* lays out a compelling case and pathway for business to help catalyze a world where all people and life can flourish. I applaud its inspiration and vision for how each of us can create the world to which we aspire for ourselves and our children."
—PAUL RICE, President and CEO, Fair Trade USA

"This book offers a clear and practical guide for anyone interested in powerfully engaging employees and outside partners in better business strategies for creativity and long-term growth."
—NICK HAMON, CEO, Innovative Vector Control Consortium

"This book recognizes that business has the power and creativity to make big things happen, to design and build a future where all life can flourish forever. This book is for anyone interested in creating such a future and in the practices that can get us there."
—ELLIOT HOFFMAN, CEO, True Market Solutions

Flourishing Enterprise

THE NEW SPIRIT OF BUSINESS

Chris Laszlo and Judy Sorum Brown

WITH
John R. Ehrenfeld, Mary Gorham,
Ilma Barros Pose, Linda Robson,
Roger Saillant, Dave Sherman,
and Paul Werder

STANFORD BUSINESS BOOKS
An Imprint of Stanford University Press
Stanford, California

Stanford University Press
Stanford, California

"Beginners" by Denise Levertov from *Candles in Babylon,* ©1982 by Denise Levertov. Reprinted by permission of New Directions Publishing Corp.

"To be of use" by Marge Piercy from *Circles on the Water: Selected Poems,* ©1973, 1982 by Marge Piercy and Middlemarsh, Inc. Used by permission of Alfred A. Knopf, an imprint of the Knopf Doubleday Publishing Group, a division of Random House LLC and Wallace Literary Agency, Inc. on behalf of Marge Piercy. All rights reserved.

"One Source of Bad Information" by Robert Bly from *Morning Poems,* ©1997, 1998 by Robert Bly. Reprinted by permission of HarperCollins Publishers and Georges Borchardt, Inc., for Robert Bly.

"Start Close In" by David Whyte from *River Flow: New & Selected Poems 1984–2007,* printed with permission from Many Rivers Press, www.davidwhyte.com. ©Many Rivers Press, Langley, Washington.

"The Appointment" by Mark Nepo reprinted with the permission of Atria Publishing Group and Mark Nepo from the Free Press edition of *Seven Thousand Ways to Listen: Staying Close to What Is Sacred* by Mark Nepo. Copyright © 2012 by Mark Nepo. All rights reserved.

Special discounts for bulk quantities of Stanford Business Books are available to corporations, professional associations, and other organizations. For details and discount information, contact the special sales department of Stanford University Press.
Tel: (650) 736-1782, Fax: (650) 736-1784

Library of Congress Cataloging-in-Publication Data

Laszlo, Christopher, author.
 Flourishing enterprise : the new spirit of business / Chris Laszlo and Judy Sorum Brown ; with John R. Ehrenfeld, Mary Gorham, Ilma Barros Pose, Linda Robson, Roger Saillant, Dave Sherman, and Paul Werder.
  pages cm
 Includes bibliographical references and index.
 ISBN 978-0-8047-8913-4 (cloth : alk. paper)
 1. Social responsibility of business. 2. Industrial management—Moral and ethical aspects. 3. Spirituality. I. Brown, Judy, 1945- author. II. Ehrenfeld, John, author. III. Gorham, Mary (Professional coach), author. IV. Barros-Pose, Ilma, author. V. Robson, Linda (Doctoral student), author. VI. Saillant, Roger, author. VII. Sherman, Dave (Executive), author. VIII. Werder, Paul, author. IX. Title.
 HD60.L367 2014
 658.4'08--dc23

 ISBN 978-0-8047-9350-6 (electronic)

Printed in the United States of America on acid-free, archival-quality paper

Typeset by Bruce Lundquist in 10.75/16 Sabon

Contents

Foreword

At last, a book focused on one of the real questions.

Years ago, William O'Brien, a very successful CEO and mentor to many of us, said:

> I go all around talking with people about values-based, vision-driven businesses. People are always very enthusiastic. It seems as if most people, once given a bit of time to consider this, are quick to declare that, indeed, this is the type of enterprise they want to be part of. This raises an obvious question: If everyone really wants this, why are such businesses so rare? I have come to conclude that most people have no idea of the nature of the commitment required to build such an organization.

Amid the tidal wave of books on sustainable business that have appeared over the past few years, we could readily ask, in the spirit of O'Brien, with so many arguments in favor of green businesses, why are we so far from such enterprises being the norm rather than the exception? Perhaps, as O'Brien suggested many years ago, we are still dancing on the surface of what it takes to build such an enterprise. Maybe the logic of the business case is just not enough, nor the compelling urgency of the societal need, nor the countless examples of good practice. Maybe we simply have not been asking the right questions: How important is this to us? And what is required of those who seek to lead in transforming vision into reality?

The project that led to this book suggests that one answer lies in connecting sustainability and spirituality. I have long found that in Western society we shy away from the word *spirituality,* mostly for fear of its association with organized religion. (I find this is less of a problem in Eastern societies.) Nonetheless, I have long noticed that very practical managers have little trouble with questions like, Have you ever been part of a team that had real spirit? or What have you learned about developing spirit, trust, and commitment within a group of people working together? It seems the phenomenon is far less scary than the abstraction. Indeed, the former strikes most experienced leaders as an essential matter, while the latter remains optional or even problematic for many.

Fortunately, in my experience, the former is the gateway to addressing O'Brien's challenge. How do we tap passion, energy, imagination, perseverance and willingness to truly grow as a human being, in ourselves and collectively? How do we recognize and cultivate people's innate sense of concern for matters beyond themselves? How do we connect this concern and willingness to creating products, processes, and business models that address the major issues of our time—food, water, energy, waste and toxicity, youth underemployment and unemployment, and the widening gap between rich and poor?

These are the types of questions that I believe could get businesses out of neutral regarding sustainability. They offer channels of deep inquiry that could mobilize energy and a sense of possibility in what is all too often a "follow the other guy" industry of modest changes that inspire modest commitment. There are no shortages of great ideas to latch onto, once we have started to light the fires waiting to be lit. There are already countless smaller enterprises creating new businesses around these questions, and a small but growing number of large global businesses, such as Nike, which is committed to zero waste, zero toxins and complete closed loop manufacture by 2020," and Unilever, which has transformed itself over the past decade and a half from a sleepy noninnovative, nongrowth company into one of Europe's most dynamic, attractive employers, and whose core strategy—its Sustainable Living Plan—involves doubling sales this decade while reducing the company's environmental footprint in absolute terms and bringing millions of "small holders" into its global food chains. Unilever CEO Paul

Polman bluntly and regularly reminds us that you cannot grow a healthy business in an unhealthy society.

Being true to its pragmatic imperative can also enable a business to overcome what I see as the primary problem with the word *spirituality*, which is too often heard as a matter of beliefs and convictions rather than practices. Practices that shift how we think and interact will help people both in getting things accomplished and in shifting the place from which we operate in our accomplishing. There are many who see themselves as spiritual people who are seen as a bit less so by those who observe their actions. It is only through practices that we can break down deep individual and collective habits, which is why half of this book is devoted to practices at the individual, team, organization, and system levels.

Having railed about "spirituality," I should add that I do not much like the word *sustainability* either, nor its more politically correct cousin, *sustainable development*. Besides being ambiguous, these words tell us only that we have a problem to solve—we are "unsustainable"—but they stir little in the mind or soul toward its solving. My ambivalence for the term was crystallized many years ago when I heard green chemist Michael Braungart say, "If someone asked you how your marriage was and you said, 'It's sustainable,' this would not be a good thing." As a rallying cry, *sustainability* fails O'Brien's test question miserably. It inspires not an inkling of understanding of the nature of the commitment needed to move reality toward the vision—indeed, for many it subtly suggests that the costs will be great and the eventual reality quite uninspiring.

Sustainability is a bit like visiting relatives who have overstayed their welcome. Politeness compels you to attend to them, but you worry that the more you do, the longer they are likely to stay. I for one am ready to stop attending and hope that we will awake one day, sooner rather than later, to discover that we simply do not need the word any longer—the unwanted relatives will have moved on.

But I am now illustrating the very sin I am complaining about. I am pointing out the problem and failing completely to evoke a sense of a solution. To correct myself, let me try it this way. There is no way we will shift the overall course of our society unless we begin to see a future that is more inspiring than the past, more in line with what we deeply care about, and more exciting than business as usual. We cannot overcome lack of commitment with better analysis.

Words matter. In seeking to animate a latent cause so vital to our future, we must find our way to articulating a purpose that taps our genuine aspirations and inspires our bountiful imaginations. No less a master of English than George Bernard Shaw said it: "This is the true joy in life, the being used for a purpose recognized by yourself as a mighty one; . . . the being a force of nature rather than a feverish, selfish little clod of ailments and grievances complaining that the world will not devote itself to making you happy.[1]" An indicator of real progress in our mission may be letting go of the negative vision of "not being unsustainable" for a positive vision—like "flourishing."

Perhaps this book can help us start to do just that. I applaud the authors' courage in tackling questions that really matter—such as "What do we call that which we are seeking to create?" and "What is the nature of commitment to our own awakening required by the undertaking?"

At the very least, this book will help readers think more deeply about these questions. At best, it may help us lose the dimly lit path we are now slogging along in favor of a truer one.

Peter Senge, Cambridge, Massachusetts, May 2014

Flourishing Enterprise

CHAPTER I

From Sustainability
to Flourishing

Why are so many executives struggling with corporate sustainability? To answer this question, a fresh outlook is needed. We start by recognizing that what is usually projected under the heading of *sustainability* has, by any measure, become insufficient for either business or society. Sustainability-related practices have implicitly focused, whether intentionally or not, on what business can do to mitigate harm or avoid disaster. In other words, the primary attention has been on being less bad. Imagine for a moment that the physicians' Hippocratic Oath was to hurt the patient less rather than to do no harm. We'd be in a world of hurt! Yet corporate sustainability initiatives such as cutting greenhouse gases or reducing waste only help a business be "less unsustainable." Few initiatives today are designed with solutions to global challenges in mind, and fewer still fulfill the systemic conditions for a healthy world over the long term.

Even the growing social entrepreneurship movement, which aims to provide innovative solutions to global sustainability challenges, is having limited success in making a world-changing impact. Although motivated by social rather than economic gain, this movement is challenged to find ways to scale impact, in part because of the inherent growth limitations linked to capital funding in small organizations that are heavily dependent on a founder's vision for success.

What if, instead of aiming primarily at reducing their footprint, businesses adopted a different way of thinking: what if, rather than only reducing their negative impacts, they started to think in terms of having a *positive handprint,* which Australian activist Kathryn Bottrell defines as "a mark and measure of making a positive contribution in the world?[1]" What would this look like?

The Tata Group, an Indian conglomerate founded in 1868 with current sales of $100 billion, is one among a growing number of examples that exist today. This company puts making a positive contribution at the core of its reason for being. Its corporate purpose of "improving the quality of life of the communities we serve" and "returning to society what we earn" forms the basis of its business conduct. Karambir Singh Kang, an executive at Taj Hotels, a division of the Tata Group, says this about his company: "You will not find the names of our leaders among the names of the richest people in the world. We have no one on the *Forbes* list. Our leaders are not in it for themselves; they are in it for society, for the communities they serve."[2] For some observers the paradox of Tata's way of doing business is the extraordinary results that come with it, most recently under its chairman, Ratan Tata, who transformed the group into a highly profitable global powerhouse over the past twenty years.[3] Its portfolio of products now includes a $22 water purifier that works without electricity or the need for running water, designed to serve the nearly one billion people worldwide who lack access to clean water. As *Wired Magazine* put it, with such products "Tata is saving lives and making a killing."[4]

Or consider Natura, the Brazilian natural cosmetics company with an innovative sales network of more than one million people, many of them poor residents of urban slums known as *favelas*. Chosen in 2011 by *Forbes* magazine as the eighth most innovative company in the world (in the company of Apple, which ranked fifth, and Google, which ranked seventh),[5] Natura has always operated from a distinct and deeply felt sense of purpose. Its founder, Luiz Seabra, says, "At age 16, I was given this quote from Plotinus, a philosopher: 'The one is in the whole; the whole is in the one.' That was a revelation to me. This notion of being part of a whole has never left me."[6] Natura's corporate purpose is concisely stated: Well-Being and Being Well. The company's goal is to cultivate healthy, transparent, positive relationships—between the company and its stakeholders, among those stakeholders, and between them and the whole system of which they are a part. Although the firm is not widely known outside of South America, it provides a formidable example of a company that does well by doing good, with a recent net profit of $440 million on annual sales of more than $3 billion.

Why Today's Sustainability Results Disappoint

Yet for all the success of companies like Tata and Natura, across a broad range of firms there is a surprising gap between executive talk about sustainability and the ability to actually create value from it. Data from a joint study conducted by the *MIT Sloan Management Review* and the Boston Consulting Group suggest that as early as 2011, two-thirds of all companies believed that sustainability was a source of competitive advantage.[7] This awareness of sustainability as a driver of business value appears encouraging, but a more sobering statistic shows that only a third of the respondents actually reaped financial profits from efforts toward sustainability. A 2011 McKinsey global survey of 3,200 executives shows similar results, with 73 percent saying it is now a priority on their CEO agenda, but less than 15 percent of respondents citing return on capital levers over the next five years.[8]

Even though corporate sustainability initiatives are more widespread now than in previous years, they are often diluted or appear to be flagging. Many of the niche pioneers of the 1970s and 1980s have been absorbed by big players, as in the case of Ben & Jerry's (Unilever) and The Body Shop (L'Oréal). Global corporations that promised to make sustainability a part of everything they did seem to have been unable to stay the course, either because of spectacular crises such as BP's Deepwater Horizon disaster in the Gulf of Mexico or because of leadership changes and confusion about focus,[9] leading to "sustainability fatigue." Whether the fatigue is the result of the "bloom being off the rose," a sense that attention to sustainability is "just one more thing on my overfull plate," or a sense that it was, sadly, just another flavor of the month, the initial energy behind the movement seems to have dissipated, despite all the public statements about the importance of sustainability. We must tap into a different level of energy and a persistent commitment in order to reinvigorate corporate efforts.

A Shareholder Perspective

Our individual and collective work with executives across a wide range of companies led us to observe that sustainability initiatives have typically begun outside their core strategy and business planning processes, and having begun thus, it has later been difficult to make those initiatives part of the organizations' core cultures, routines, and strategies. In tough economic times tangential efforts naturally fall by the wayside. But even in good times they suffer from being peripheral and from drawing only sporadic attention.

Organizations typically go through several phases in their sustainability efforts. First they identify activities they are already doing that can be couched in sustainability terms. They frame and communicate these efforts in corporate social responsibility (CSR) reports, at conferences, and in their press releases. They look for efforts that are newsworthy, even when many (such as a small solar installation at the entrance of an energy-intensive manufacturing facility) may not have significant impact overall.

Next, they begin tracking performance against key indicators and looking for ways to improve their sustainability performance. Here success typically comes in areas that are consistent with the company's pre-existing culture and ways of operating. For example, Walmart had significant early success with cost-saving efforts, such as introducing innovations to improve the energy efficiency of its buildings and truck fleet and reducing the amount of packaging in its own-branded products.

However, sustainability efforts often run into trouble when they conflict with current ways of operating and require new levels of collaboration both within the organization and with outsiders (such as other industry players or value chain partners). Walmart faced significant challenges partnering with suppliers to bring more sustainable products to market. This is in part because the "buyer" culture (based on the company having massive purchasing power over its suppliers) favored price negotiation rather than innovative and long-term partnerships. In a 2011 interview published in the *Wall Street Journal,* the head of Walmart's U.S. division responded to criticism that the company had "lost its way a bit" and was no longer as focused as it needed to be on offering the lowest possible prices. He reported that "sustainability and some of these other initiatives can be distracting."[10] While former CEO Lee Scott saw sustainability as a true paradigm shift for the company, this divisional executive's words suggest that the established cultural norms and ways of doing things exert strong pressure to return to the status quo.

Given this tug of war between old and new, and the widespread but inaccurate assumption that by their very nature sustainability efforts take a long time to produce profits, shareholders seemed to have good reason to be disappointed. With investors disgruntled, why should management risk what could appear to be a weakly performing sustainability agenda?

A Stakeholder Perspective

When we turn to stakeholders—particularly the citizens and organizations who fight for social and environmental causes—the picture is even more disappointing. All meaningful indicators suggest that major systems across the world are becoming at best *less un*sustainable and at worst we are heading toward major crises. Progress toward the Millennium Development Goals is mixed.[11] Poverty and the gap between the rich and the poor are growing, even in high-income countries; and progress toward improving maternal health and reducing child mortality is stalled in many parts of the world.

According to the UN's Food and Agriculture Organization (FAO), chronic hunger has been steadily rising since the mid-1990s and in 2012 affected 900 million people worldwide.[12] Efforts to become more environmentally sustainable, as measured by reversing forest loss and

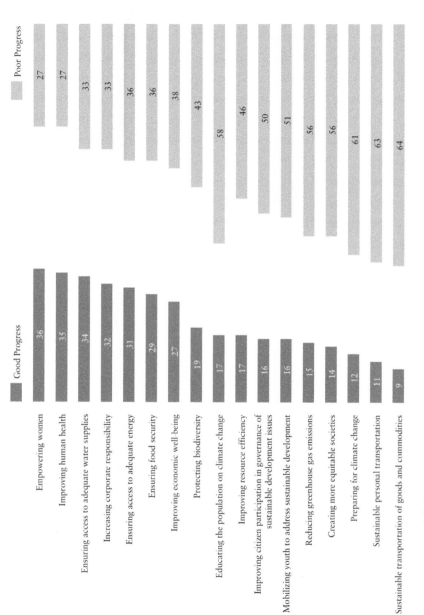

Good Progress

Empowering women	36
Improving human health	35
Ensuring access to adequate water supplies	34
Increasing corporate responsibility	32
Ensuring access to adequate energy	31
Ensuring food security	29
Improving economic well being	27
Protecting biodiversity	19
Educating the population on climate change	17
Improving resource efficiency	17
Improving citizen participation in governance of sustainable development issues	16
Mobilizing youth to address sustainable development	16
Reducing greenhouse gas emissions	15
Creating more equitable societies	14
Preparing for climate change	12
Sustainable personal transportation	11
Sustainable transportation of goods and commodities	9

Poor Progress

Empowering women	27
Improving human health	27
Ensuring access to adequate water supplies	33
Increasing corporate responsibility	33
Ensuring access to adequate energy	36
Ensuring food security	36
Improving economic well being	38
Protecting biodiversity	43
Educating the population on climate change	58
Improving resource efficiency	46
Improving citizen participation in governance of sustainable development issues	50
Mobilizing youth to address sustainable development	51
Reducing greenhouse gas emissions	56
Creating more equitable societies	56
Preparing for climate change	61
Sustainable personal transportation	63
Sustainable transportation of goods and commodities	64

FIGURE 1.1 Global Expert Perspectives on the State of Sustainable Development

SOURCE: GlobeScan SustainAbility Survey of 1600 Sustainable Experts. Last accessed 09/23/2012.

reducing the proportion of the population without access to clean drinking water, are faltering in many regions. In climate-change terms, carbon dioxide emissions grew by 2.07 percent in 2013, increasing the total amount of atmospheric carbon to 400 parts per million.[13] To provide historical perspective, atmospheric carbon stood at around 280 ppm for the last million years as measured by ice core samples. By 2013, atmospheric carbon had surpassed 400 ppm,[14] a level that many see as putting us at risk for catastrophic climate change.[15]

In a 2012 survey conducted by SustainAbility and GlobeScan, 1,603 experts worldwide, drawn from corporate, government, non-governmental, academic, media, and other organizations, responded to a series of questions regarding the progress of sustainable development (SD) in the past two decades.[16] As Figure 1.1 shows, only three of seventeen indicators (empowering women, improving human health, and ensuring access to adequate water supplies) were perceived to have made slightly more "good progress" than "poor progress" over the past two decades. Several grievous problems, such as protecting biodiversity and creating more equitable societies, were estimated to have worsened significantly.

Poor progress is seen not only in terms of social equity. It also encompasses practical realities that businesses already care deeply about, such as improving resource efficiency and providing sustainable transportation of goods and commodities.

In light of these poor shareholder and stakeholder outcomes, to claim that business, as an institution, is materially contributing to a more sustainable world seems increasingly far-fetched. Could the idea of sustainability—the very term—be responsible for the poor results we observe? Are companies such as Tata and Natura, which are bucking these trends, actually doing something else? We argue that they are.

Book Tour by Chapter

Let us walk you through the territory ahead. Chapter 1 reframes sustainability as flourishing and outlines what we mean by the new spirit of business. Chapter 2 provides the historical context, including the external market forces and internal motives that are driving a spiritual dimension into all enterprise. It examines our increased collective desire for meaning and our rising awareness that business is not contributing to environmental, health, and social sustainability at a larger scale. The foundation for our work is developed further in Chapter 3, which together with Chapter 4 provides a bridge between the concepts and actual practices aimed at flourishing. These reflective practices are described in Chapters 5 through 7, according to whether they are aimed primarily at the individual, at the organization, or at the systems level. Chapter 8 serves as a conclusion and as an invitation for further exploration.

Management has long concerned itself with individual motivation, commitment, and tenacity in the workforce. In recent years interest has deepened in areas such as emotional intelligence. Many theories of leadership take into account the affective states, that is, the moods and emotions of the people involved. Our contribution is to suggest that a range of reflective practices, some of which may be seen as spiritual (whether they have their roots in spiritual tradition or not), can facilitate the emergence of individual awareness of connection and the need for caring (for self, others, and the world). These practices foster a richer sense of creativity, which is critical for any enterprise to flourish. It is by tapping into the spiritual dimension that we are able to reach the threshold of an enduringly systemic view of sustainability. At the heart of this transformation is an awareness of connectedness between the world of human beings and all other forms of life.

Redefining Sustainability as Flourishing

If the term *sustainability* has run out of steam, we need not only a better meaning but a better word, one that points to fresh practices and the possibility of far better results. For us, as well as for a growing number of renowned thought leaders,[17] the right word is much more ambitious: *flourishing*. Flourishing at all levels—individual, team, organizational, and global. Think of flourishing relationships, radiant health, thriving enterprises, and humming communities.

Flourishing is not anchored in mundane notions of continuity. It is not about passing along what is now available. Giving future generations the opportunities faced by the current generation may not mean much if all we now have is the prospect of bleak material survival. Instead, flourishing is about the world for which we all yearn. It's about "thriving," "doing well," and "prospering" (according to the Collins English Thesaurus[18]) and about "growing or developing in a healthy or vigorous way, especially as the result of a particularly congenial environment" (Oxford Dictionary[19]).

Our challenge is to realize and acknowledge how much we are caged in by ideas that are no longer working for us,[20] and to begin to see what can be made possible with the power of new words and new practices.

The word *flourishing* has the power to engage a broad range of people, from leaders to front-line employees and supply chain partners, in a way that *sustainability* simply does not. Companies that can see *flourishing* in their vision and mission are able to engage fully the potential of everyone in the company and to attract the best partners and stakeholders while also reducing employee turnover. Employees in and partners of flourishing organizations are better at working together and are more creative and innovative. They build stronger relationships with customers, who in turn do much of the marketing on the company's behalf. These kinds of benefits allow companies to deal better with the realities of a complex and volatile world.

Whole Foods co-CEO Walter Robb talks about the importance of giving employees a powerful and inspiring purpose:

I always ask new Team Members how and why they have come to work for us. After what at this point are thousands of individual conversations, I can tell you that besides our reputation for being a good place to work, the single most important reason is that we line up with their own personal values and that they truly feel we are a place where they can make a difference in the world.[21]

Marcelo Cardoso, a senior vice president at Natura, told us,

We started by creating space to talk about meaning and purpose. It was an opportunity to reflect about legacy: What is each person's purpose in life that is greater than their own existence? What would allow them to die with a sense of integrity that their life was worth living? Asking this question to your employees and challenging them around how they can begin creating their purpose now will have tremendous impact on their lives and ultimately on their performance.

Clearly the idea of *thriving* is quite different from that of *surviving*—in part because flourishing must be at the core of the organization's purpose. It has such a profound ripple effect that it cannot become the side initiative that sustainability has been. We invite you to join with us in awakening and motivating organizations to work toward "the possibility that humans and other life can flourish on earth forever."[22] It was this definition of flourishing, offered by John Ehrenfeld, this reframing of sustainability, that created resonance among those of us who wrote this book. Pursuing a 150-year vision in addition to the typical three- or five-year plan puts an organization on the path of immense and important work. We will need to redesign our economic systems, to change laws and policies, and to find vast new opportunities for businesses to generate sustainable value. This undertaking can quickly feel overwhelming, but don't panic. Many people around the world are already at work on this important task and many more are waiting to be engaged in the social movement that is presently under way, as described by Paul Hawken in his bestseller *Blessed Unrest*.[23]

Where do we begin? A first step is right in front of us. We need to recall how to flourish as individuals, not just economically but in every dimension of life, including in what some would call the domain of our hearts. Amy Spatrisano, a principal at the sustainable meeting management firm MeetGreen and cofounder of the Green Meeting Industry Council, shared with us her initial apprehension about entering this "soft" domain. "Originally, 'speaking from the heart' was a foreign concept in relationship to business that caused my palms to sweat. I'd quickly change the subject since nowhere in my learning about business success had I been taught to include compassion or anything connected to it. What I realize now is I'd been missing the immense power of engagement and enrollment that such practices offer. We have consistently seen our contribution expand, with incredible results, when we are coming from our hearts."

Many of the business leaders and scholars we interviewed shared with us their own realization that something was missing for them in the business equation. Like us, they sensed that the missing piece of the puzzle might lie in the dimension of spirituality, connection, and caring for others. We know from research and our own experience that many business people who as individuals are caring feel unable to bring their whole selves to their work. People often joke about having to leave their nobler half outside the office door, but that missing half contains their creativity, heart, spirit, and personal integrity. Having left those qualities at the door, they wrestle with business decisions in ways that may be in conflict with how they think about what is important. In the culture of business, as they experience it, such conflicted decisions are too often the norm. In some cases, organizations are simply missing the richness of people's thinking and experience. In more troublesome cases, the organizations end up in a public crisis that literally strips them of value as a result of people being unable to stand up for what they believe.

What We Mean by Spirituality

How can we talk sensibly and practically, at work, about spirituality? Having explored the broader meaning of sustainability as flourishing, we turn now to the frequently mysterious and often troublesome term *spirituality* as it is currently used in the context of business and as it might serve our quest for flourishing.

As many business practitioners reminded us, the word *spirituality* is fraught with ambiguity and misconception. It can sound "new-agey" to those who are religious, and misguided and even like infringing on personal liberties to the nonreligious. For others it is too soft to be practical for the bottom-line mindset that prevails in the corporate world, even though, as we show in this book, it is key to very tangible business benefits. For anyone intent on understanding the role of spirituality in shaping our lives, our careers, and our organizations while not necessarily wanting to enter into a conversation about spirituality for its own sake, we hope to give you a definition that is universal, accessible, and relevant. We provide language and a conceptual meaning that are intended to be both precise and "safe" to use at work.

Spiritual leadership pioneers Danah Zohar and Ian Marshall provide a good introductory definition of spirituality. They begin by drawing on "Webster's" dictionary definition of spirit—"the vital principle or animating force traditionally believed to be the intangible, life affirming force in self and all human beings". They go on to define spirituality as "to be in touch with some larger, deeper, richer whole that puts our present limited situation into a new perspective.[24]" Louis W. Fry proposes two key ideas that ultimately became the foundation for much of our own work: the *search for meaning* and *consciousness of interconnectedness*. On the basis of these two ideas, Fry defines spirituality as "the source for one's search for meaning in life and a sense of interconnectedness with other beings."[25]

This definition is echoed in an empirical study by Ian Mitroff and Elizabeth Denton, published in the *MIT Sloan Management Review,* in which interviewees drawn mostly from business organizations defined spirituality as "the basic feeling of being connected with one's complete self, others, and the entire universe."[26] Mitroff and Denton conclude: "If a single word best captures the meaning of spirituality and the vital role that it plays in people's lives, that word is 'interconnectedness.'"[27]

We build on the work of these researchers as well as on our interviews with business executives and thought leaders to define spirituality as *a way of experiencing the world and taking action that leads to caring, based on a personal quest for connectedness and meaning.* Such an orientation can lead to a more relationship-based way of experiencing the world, which in turn enables actions that support flourishing enterprise. It is an orientation that contributes (and adds energy) to the reinforcing loop of caring, commitment, and calling, which makes it quite different from the analytic learning behind the business case for sustainability, or the emotional and moral appeal for greater responsibility.

A case in point: Jon Coleman, director of marketing and sales at Ford Motor Company, sees authentic action that demonstrates strong values as one way that spirituality contributes to more powerful ways of doing business. In our interview with him, he said that when he finds potential customer companies that have strong values (for example, Merck and its focus on water), he looks for ways that he can demonstrate values alignment as one of the foundations of a stronger partner relationship. This approach goes beyond costs to something deeper and stronger. Says Coleman, "If sustainability is viewed only from a cost savings and efficiency point of view, then the opportunities are limited. But if it is viewed from a creativity and innovation perspective, the sky is the limit."

How Is Spirituality Different from Religion?

This is a thorny question for many readers. Volumes could be (and have been) written on the topic, but here we content ourselves with a brief but powerful distinction offered by the Dalai Lama:

Religion I take to be concerned with faith in the claims to salvation of one faith tradition or another, an aspect of which is the acceptance of some form of heaven or nirvana. Connected with this are religious teachings or dogma, ritual prayer, and so on. Spirituality I take to be concerned with those qualities of the human spirit—such as love and compassion, patience, tolerance, forgiveness, contentment, a sense of responsibility, a sense of harmony—which brings happiness to both self and others.[28]

Clearly one does not exclude the other. Religion attempts to embrace spirituality at its roots. There is a growing movement of faith at work, which in many ways parallels the increased interest in spirituality in the workplace. Readers who have a strong faith-based approach to pursuing the search for meaning and connectedness will naturally want to explore flourishing from a faith-based perspective.

Our choice to frame the book's discussion in terms of spirituality instead of religion is based on a desire to be inclusive and to make business engagement in these matters more natural and accessible. Whatever the nature or extent of the faith you follow, even if you do not subscribe to any faith tradition, this book can offer powerful ways to engage yourself and others on the journey to flourishing.

Putting the Domain of Spirituality into Common Language

How can we talk of spirituality in a work setting? How do we stay out of the ditch and away from the landmines? What language works best for people? In our interviews and research, we found that people use a variety of words to point to essentially the same thing. A business leader worked to cultivate an environment in which employees could experience a sense of *connectedness* with others and with nature. A scholar studied how the *meaning* of one's work often comes from experiences that *transcend* it. A colleague taught a course on *self-management,* "managing your insides so you can deal with your outsides better."[29] A consultant guided clients to uncovering their *inner wisdom.* An entrepreneur called it *presence,* a leadership writer called it *spirit,* and a manager called it *faith.* Although the labels people use differ, the experiences described have much more in common than the diversity of their expression would suggest.

The *Handbook of Workplace Spirituality and Organizational Performance* provides a representative sampling of fourteen definitions of spirituality and summarizes ten definitional components on the basis of an extensive literature review.[30] One of the more highly

cited scholarly articles identified the following components of spirituality: Conditions for Community, Meaning at Work, Inner Life,
Personal Responsibility, Positive Connections with Others, and Behaviors Associated with Expressing Inner Life.[31] You can see the range
of concepts and terms that fall under this topic heading. Which ones
can you imagine having power in your workplace? And how can
you act on the multiplicity of ideas that the people you work with
already possess?

We have come to think of spirituality as the meeting point of
many paths, each of which has a different name. Like the spokes of
a bicycle wheel, some points on these paths are further apart than
others, but where they converge we find people from different backgrounds and walks of life resonating. At this point of convergence,
we discover profound experiences that give life to the idea of personal
flourishing while contributing to a thriving business and a healthy
world. We have tried to capture aspects of these experiences and the
practices that lead to that "hub." We share them in detail in later
chapters, but the precise, powerful, and provocative language that
encompasses those experiences and practices—for which we use the
term *spirituality*—remains elusive. The Sufi poet Rumi expresses the
difficulty of finding language for that convergence:[32]

Out Beyond Ideas

Out beyond ideas of wrongdoing and rightdoing,
there is a field. I'll meet you there.

When the soul lies down in that grass,
the world is too full to talk about.
Ideas, language, even the phrase *each other*
doesn't make any sense.

How can we engage a broad swath of people in tapping into spirituality and pursuing flourishing when we see the world so differently
from one another?

The Transcendent and Immanent Paths
to Spiritual Experience

Our approach to spirituality, inclusive as it is, still runs the risk of distancing some people. Those who have deep religious beliefs and would prefer to see flourishing enterprise placed under the *faith at work* heading may feel excluded. One executive, a president and CEO of several companies, said of our project, "Personally, I was put off by what I perceived as a more Eastern, New Age orientation of spirituality. There is a whole body of literature in the Christian community encouraging followers of Christ to live out their faith at work and, in fact, many Christians are doing just that—using biblical principles in the way they conduct themselves at work."

At the other end of the spectrum, a seasoned executive we interviewed felt that his personal orientation comes from a deep connection to nature and does not reflect a spiritual practice, and our approach left him feeling "outside the tent." This business of building a tent of the right size turns out to be very complicated and yet, when done right, it can be stable and weather-worthy. Over time, our broad approach has come to cover a lot of ground and invite in many people.

We see two broad paths to spiritual experience, which can be termed the *transcendent* and the *immanent*. The transcendent path results from recognition of the existence of a transcendent force or being, a divine and sacred source that many people call God. That force is experienced through an epiphany or contact with the non-material world.[33] Implicit in this concept is the notion that spiritual meaning comes from somewhere other than the physical world, from a pure, eternal dimension.

The second path, the path of immanence, is rooted in an appreciation of the oneness and interconnectedness of the world around us. The notion of immanence sees evidence of the spiritual dimension within the material dimension of our lives, so that spiritual meaning and experience are ever present within and around us.[34] Kentucky farmer-poet Wendell Berry captures the essence of the immanent path in his poem "The Peace of Wild Things."[35]

When despair for the world grows in me
and I wake in the night at the least sound
in fear of what my life and my children's lives may be,
I go and lie down where the wood drake
rests in his beauty on the water, and the great heron feeds.
I come into the peace of wild things
who do not tax their lives with forethought
of grief. I come into the presence of still water.
And I feel above me the day-blind stars
waiting with their light. For a time
I rest in the grace of the world, and am free.

With immanence there are at least two possible explanations for experiences that the perceiver deems spiritual. One is that, although the experience is clearly present, it has no ascribable origin in the external world. The other explanation is that the person has "tuned into" some universal field that cannot be measured by current means, but for which there is reasonable science-based conjecture. Insights emerging from the new sciences, such as quantum mechanics and evolutionary biology, suggest that the fabric of the physical universe is an interconnecting and coherence-producing field rather than inert clumps of atoms in an empty vacuum.[36] Other disciplines such as the brain sciences as well as the beliefs of indigenous peoples throughout history suggest that consciousness may be a universal property and not limited to individual human beings. The universal field explanation can be logically extended to include a sense of interconnectedness, because fields are by definition constituted by action at a distance, which is the same as implying that physically separate objects are connected.

For some, transcendence and immanence are positioned as dualities, with one perspective chosen over the other. Others see them as polarities—paradoxical notions that can be held simultaneously. We suggest, for the purpose of our project, that the differences between transcendence and immanence are more reflective of how people habitually process the world and of the cultural or spiritual worldview in which they operate than of any fundamental division. We hold that both transcendence and immanence can explain a consciousness of connectedness and a striving for oneness, but they simply do so in different ways.[37]

A Definition of Spirituality for Flourishing Enterprise

It was our attempt to describe the meeting point in Rumi's poem that produced our image of the spokes on a wheel and leads us to frame the cycling of this wheel as an exploration with signposts:

1. Intentional practices such as meditation that
2. serve to integrate and align our hearts, minds, and behaviors
3. leading to an observable expression of a mindful path that
4. incorporates the processes of *inquiry, appreciation,* and *discovery* as ways to engage and empower others to bring their whole selves into their participation in a larger system.

In the course of our research, through both interviews and studies of existing methods for engaging people in such exploration, we began to frame these ideas as a set of questions:

To what extent am I undertaking a personal or collective exploration that

connects with my complete self, others, and the larger world around me?

creates increasing degrees of calm, wisdom, peace, and love?

To what extent would others say of me, from observing my behavior, that

> I live from qualities such as personal responsibility, commitment, gratitude, compassion, patience, tolerance, forgiveness, contentment, and a sense of harmony with my environment?

> I live from the "golden rule" (or its equivalent)?

> I am in altruistic service to others?

Questions like these guided Robert Greenleaf, an AT&T executive who half a century ago formulated a leadership framework known as Servant Leadership.[38] The hard-nosed organizations that successfully followed his guidance include The Toro Company, ServiceMaster, Southwest Airlines, and TDIndustries.

Practical Value in Leadership and General Management

We have explored the dynamic and complementary relationship between connectedness (our shorthand for an essential dimension of spirituality) and sustainability (which we have redefined as flourishing). This exploration can be seen as supported by both transcendent and immanent models of the world. We see these models as offering dynamic and complementary paths to individual experiences and to awareness that is essential for business to contribute to a prosperous and flourishing world. We point later to reflective practices, some explicitly spiritual, others less so, that can be seen as essential to flourishing.

What changes when such a fresh perspective is adopted by individuals and organizational cultures? When a business shifts its sustainability goals from *reducing harm* to *creating prosperity and flourishing,* it assumes a greater purpose and responsibility for the health and well-being of a complex whole. The goal of flourishing cannot be pursued using familiar reductionist modes of thinking and acting. We can no longer assume that it is feasible to solve sustainability problems in one part of the value chain without taking into account the sustainability impacts across the whole product life cycle. We can no longer assume the inexhaustibility of all natural resources. We must reconsider the idea that economic growth and wealth are the sole measures of well-being.

For a business to embed sustainability as flourishing in its strategy and operations requires a transformation of its workforce and of the many stakeholders outside the organization. Everyone from top to bottom will need to develop the capacity to feel, see, and act differently. This shift calls for the development of a broader perception, a greater sense of connectedness to the community and to the rest of the world. It requires us to draw on wisdom that will lead to natural and automatic caring for others and for all of life. This sense of connection and caring, as if together we are part of a single home, is reflected in the following words and images by Judy Sorum Brown:[39]

Trilliums

He said to me

That sometimes

When he's in the woods

In springtime,

And the trilliums are blooming,

He disappears.

Completely.

He is gone

Into the whole of things,

Lost

In the universe

Of which he is

A breathing part.

Gone home.

When the world feels like our home, the connection and caring that are evoked in us present remarkable new possibilities. While some business leaders might see such notions of caring as too emotional or only for human resource professionals, an increasing number of CEOs are beginning to espouse their practical value in leadership and in general management. "Caring is not a sign of weakness," says former Starbucks president Howard Behar, "but rather a sign of strength, and it can't be faked—within an organization, with the people we serve, or in the local or global community. Without trust and caring we'll never know what could have been possible. . . . we can't dream and we can't reach our potential."[40] When our goal is flourishing, caring becomes more vital than ever to enterprise success.

The business leader's role becomes one of creating work environments where people can experience a deeper sense of connection to, and care for, others and the world around them. Such work environments serve as the nutrient-rich soil for a more enlightened form of business acumen that is necessary to grow a flourishing organization. We invite you to explore with us the reasons for the current surge in interest and growing relevance of these ideas and the practices that support them.

CHAPTER 2

Why This, Why Now?

Some lines from Denise Levertov's poem "Beginnings" offer a way to understand the importance of this moment.[1]

> We have only begun
> To imagine the fullness of life.
> How could we tire of hope?
> —so much is in bud. . . .
> We have only begun to know
> The power that is in us if we would join
> Our solitudes in the communion of struggle.
> So much is unfolding that must
> Complete its gesture,
> So much is in bud.

The timing of this book reflects a rapidly growing social movement in business: people seeking to find more meaning and to feel more connected to purpose, to others, and to the natural world. In *Megatrends 2010: The Rise of Conscious Capitalism*, Patricia Aburdene goes so far as to say that the focus on spirituality in business is becoming "today's greatest megatrend."[2] Louis W. Fry points to the growing number of companies that are using spiritual lessons in their management and leadership strategies. He cites Ben & Jerry's, SREI Infrastructure Finance Limited, and BioGenenex, among many others.[3] Mitroff and Denton believe that spirituality is becoming the ultimate competitive advantage.[4] These findings are corroborated by our own experience in business and by the many interviews we did with business practitioners and thought leaders.

A convergence of forces is moving us in the direction suggested by

Mitroff and Denton. Some of these forces are evident in the historical view of management thinking and in recent shifts in that thinking. Some are evident in the external market forces that are driving businesses to embrace sustainability as a source of value creation. Others are shaped by the internal motives that are sparking people's increased desire for meaning and their longing for a more spirited life. Each of these forces is spelled out in the following sections.

Historical Foundations in Economics and Management Thinking

If we take a step back we can see how the culture of business life over many decades has been mainly silent with regard to spirituality. Outside of specialized domains such as *spiritual leadership*[5] and *faith at work,*[6] the literature and practices of management have largely ignored the spiritual dimension of individuals. Neoclassical economics, which provides a foundation for management disciplines such as corporate strategy and finance, has a strongly reductionist view of human beings as utility maximizing agents with mysteriously assigned preferences. A typical economics textbook introduces its subject as follows: "Macroeconomics . . . studies the 'big picture," the aggregate flows of resources, goods and the overall level of prices. Microeconomics . . . studies the behavior of decision makers in households, firms, and governments. . . ."[7] Today it seems natural to wonder, where in all this is individual well-being or the quality of the human experience?

The transactional theory of the firm, which Nobel Prize winner Ronald Coase developed in his 1937 seminal paper, "The Nature of the Firm," explains why individuals come together to form organizations for the purpose of conducting business. Around that time Arthur Pigou developed his theory of economic output, wealth, tax, and employment, building a model based on the sum of the marginal cost curves of firms in equilibrium with the sum of the marginal utility curves of individuals. In the work of both Coase and Pigou, important foundations were laid for considering consumers (households) and employees (labor) as relevant entities of study, yet most of these references to individuals were devoid of spiritual, emotional, and other qualities of experience.

While Coase and Pigou were establishing their models, Frederick Taylor's *Scientific Management* and Alfred Sloan's professionalization of managerial functions at General Motors treated organizational man as analogous to a cog in a machine, a cog that could be optimized through time and motion studies. Whether the person was flourishing in any nonmaterial sense was irrelevant.

In the emerging field of strategy management, the goal was to create above-industry average profits for competing firms. Strategy pioneers such as Alfred Chandler and E. P. Learned saw their main objective as developing a process of setting a company's direction (where it is going) and aligning its activities to that chosen future (how it will get there). Corporate strategy came to be seen as an *externally oriented* concept of how business achieves its objectives. Michael Porter summarized the idea as follows: "The essence of formulating competitive strategy is relating a company to its environment."[8] There were no words about the firm's purpose or meaning other than being a means to maximize profits.

The belief implicit in much of this applied body of work was that efficient markets, with the help of effective government policy, can enable firms to grow their profits and enable economies to achieve full employment, ultimately generating wealth for everyone. The experience of the Great Depression led to the successful application of macroeconomic policies such as the Keynesian accelerator effect, monetarism, and financial regulations to produce controllable economic growth.

The development of theoretical frameworks by strategy gurus such as Michael Porter and Clayton Christensen led to the further professionalization of strategy management. Notions of competitive positioning and disruptive innovation allowed companies to differentiate themselves from their competitors and to serve their customers' needs in new and unique ways.

Another emerging body of strategy theory labeled the resource-based view (RBV) of the firm has found that distinctive resources and capabilities are the key to achieving superior returns. This is particularly true for knowledge, know-how, and innovation as sources of unique advantage for companies finding ways to create value outside of established industry boundaries. This newer body of work includes a strong interest in organizational learning.

Theory development in the area of the RBV has been prolific over the past thirty years but its roots lie much earlier, beginning with Edith Penrose's classic 1959 book *The Theory of the Growth of the Firm*,[9] and it includes a large number of academic papers from the mid-1980s onward. Literally thousands of papers now explore this topic, including ones that address the role of intangible resources and capabilities such as knowledge, networks, reputation, strategic alliances, pricing processes, and collaboration. But research attention to business practices has lagged, and intangible value remains underestimated in resource allocation decisions.

A further extension of the RBV came from studying the fast pace of change in Silicon Valley. Dynamic capabilities theory was developed to understand success in fast-paced dynamic environments.[10] It was initially conceived to help explain the factors that separate success from failure for firms in the fast-changing high technology sector. Today, even sectors that until recently were considered relatively stable are facing increasingly volatile and unpredictable business environments. Rapid technological innovation is impacting more and more sectors (such as retail, finance, and travel) with disruptive effect. Given this new volatility, the dynamic capabilities approach has a much broader application than initially envisioned.

The basic proposition behind the dynamic capabilities approach is that value-creating organizations need new capabilities: the ability to sense changes in the external environment, to learn quickly, to build new strategic assets, to integrate them into the organization, and to reconfigure existing strategic assets. Hence, value-creating management teams must dynamically manage their organizations' capabilities in order to stay in sync with their changing business ecosystem.

The increasingly important roles of knowledge, collaboration, reputation, networks, and alliances highlight the growing importance of how individuals, teams, and groups interact and work together. They also point to the importance of the capacity of individuals and teams to *attune, notice,* and *sense* in a variety of ways.

A lesser known but highly important strand of strategic literature, on stakeholder theory,[11] evolved alongside RBV and dynamic capabilities. Although there is noticeable synergy between the two strands, astoundingly there has been little integration between them. Stakeholder theory points to the importance of paying attention to the real-world needs and idiosyncrasies of key constituencies.

When we turn from economics and strategy to the human side of enterprise, we begin by noting that organization development (OD) historically focused on both organizational effectiveness[12] and humanistic values.[13] The field of positive psychology, from Maslow[14] to Seligman,[15] similarly sought to unleash human potential with the goal of increasing positive emotion, engagement, meaning, positive relationships, and accomplishment. Yet both fields accorded little attention to stakeholder theory or to global issues related to sustainability. The same can be said for advances at the intersection of neuroscience and leadership, which focus on new ways to cultivate high engagement, creativity, and the resilience of individuals and teams.[16] Their advances too were made independently of any relationship to stakeholder theory or sustainability.

We note that during the same period in which the behavioral sciences were developing in a way that emphasized high performance and engagement, interest in workplace spirituality grew dramatically in the popular press as well as in academic research.[17] The Management, Spirituality and Religion Interest Group of the Academy of Management, formed in 1999, focuses on research related to the relevance and relationship of spirituality and religion in management and organizational life. The *Journal of Management, Spirituality & Religion* was established in 2004. From 1999 through 2008, 209 articles on workplace spirituality were published in all Social Science Citation Information journals, 71 of these in management journals. Fifty-five edited collections and monographs addressing spirituality at work were published during the same period.[18] The collections and monographs reflected three levels of spiritual analysis:

Individual: dealing primarily with personal well-being, personal development, and personal effectiveness

Group: dealing with spiritual leadership at a collective level

Organization: dealing with institutional and social change

Much of this growing literature makes a direct and instrumental link between spirituality and business success. Spirituality and leadership with a spiritual dimension are thought to have several important impacts: (1) fostering employee well-being; (2) supporting a sense of meaning, purpose, and calling; and (3) strengthening a sense of community and interconnectedness. These in turn lead to improved business performance.

More recently, a number of articles have aimed at the intersection of spirituality, business, and sustainability.[19] Some scholarly practitioners have argued that spirituality should be redefined in secular terms for business. Such redefinitions include the terms *spiritual intelligence* and *full-spectrum consciousness*. Other scholars have argued that spirituality should not be harnessed for organizational purposes at all, preferring not to see it exploited for business purposes.

Even at the global level, increasingly questions are being raised about how we think about business and progress. In today's world, the singular goals of economic growth and competitive advantage can seem not only elusive but of questionable desirability. A sense of looming crisis and dissatisfaction exists in both developed and developing countries. "The GDP[gross domestic product]-led development model that compels boundless growth on a planet with limited resources no longer makes economic sense," said the prime minister of one country at a 2012 U.N. conference. "The purpose of development must be to create enabling conditions through public policy for the pursuit of the ultimate goal of happiness by all citizens."[20]

The megatrends described in the following section suggest that the world around us is paying a heavy price for our single-minded focus on economic maximization. If instead the goal becomes widespread *flourishing, prosperity,* and *healthy human and natural systems,* then the questions that increasingly must drive business decisions are, What are the payoffs of that newer goal? And what are the costs of continuing to ignore the well-being and quality of individual experience in the way we approach business management and economic policy?

External Market Forces Driving Business to Embed Sustainability

During the past half century, the market conditions that executives face have changed dramatically. The business environment has become increasingly volatile and risky as widespread change has led to the emergence of new industries, global integration, disruptive innovation, and unpredictable global environmental and political dynamics. In this fast-changing and volatile context, innovation in technology, processes, products, and business models has become ever more important. Intangible resources such as know-how, reputation, and webs of networks and relationships with suppliers, customers, business partners, universities, governments, and other stakeholders have grown increasingly critical to success.

In recent years, three big trends—declining resources, radical transparency, and increasing stakeholder expectations—have helped to drive business to embed sustainability in strategy and operations.[21] Bolt-on sustainability efforts such as greening[22] or corporate social responsibility limited to charity and philanthropy are no longer sufficient for either business or society. The linear throwaway economy, in which products and services follow a one-way trajectory from extraction to use and disposal, can no longer be supported, because we are simply running out of materials to unearth and places to landfill. Consumers, employees, and investors are beginning to ask for socially and environmentally savvy products without compromise, and radical transparency is putting every company under a microscope. A new mindset and approach, going way beyond traditional sustainability efforts to slow the damage, are needed for business to thrive in the face of these emerging market realities. Let's dig into these three big trends in more detail.

Declining resources. Stark evidence of the increasingly large and disruptive risks that businesses face is outlined in the annual Global Risks Report published by the World Economic Forum in collaboration with Wharton's Center for Risk Management and several leading insurance and financial institutions.[23] The report includes both a global risk landscape and a global risk interconnection map. More than forty specific risks in categories such as economic, environmental, societal, geopolitical, and technological are identified. The key message is that the world faces a number of high-probability and large (up to one trillion dollars in impact) risks, such as geopolitical conflict, climate change, and financial crises. These risks are inextricably interdependent and interwoven. Hence a crisis in one area will quickly lead to crises in other areas. Yet our attempts at understanding these systems, let alone managing them, are fragmented. Our current, piecemeal solutions crumble in the face of these challenges. We need an orientation that provides the insights about interconnection that are key to success.

Risks with global implications coupled with declining natural resources threaten value chains in every sector, as do volatile and rising commodity prices. Perhaps most worrisome of all is the decline in biodiversity due to species extinction, which has risen to more than one thousand times the background rate over the course of the earth's history. We might be glib about the extinction of one or another insect, plant, or bird species, but if there were to be a single indicator of the health of the planet's natural systems, it would be the rate of biodiversity loss—the sum total of all impacts, brought together into a single measure of the health of living systems, including human systems, in all of their interdependencies.

Radical transparency. Fueled by unprecedented activism in the civil sector and supported by rapid developments in information technology, transparency has become an unavoidable aspect of modern corporate life. It means that any interested person or group can peer into product life cycles and find (and publicize) the impacts on society and nature that used to be hidden from public scrutiny.

Increasing stakeholder expectations. Rising market expectations invite companies to rethink the very essence of market demand. Investors, employees, and most important, consumers increasingly expect sound social and environmental performance. New parameters, such as *quiet, healthy,* and *socially equitable,* are becoming standard for every product and service in the economy. We don't want just any household cleaning product; we want it to be nontoxic and biodegradable. We drink fair trade coffee and bring reusable shopping bags to the supermarket. And we no longer find it acceptable to pay more for these attributes.

As a result of these trends, the way we do things in almost every sector, whether manufacturing, healthcare, or agriculture, must change during the course of the next few decades or the world will not be able to support the growing population and increasing standards of living to which all of us, including people in developing countries, aspire. This means that the winning companies and organizations in almost every sector will be those that innovate and contribute to finding new (and profitable) solutions to these global problems.

Even in sectors that have traditionally been slow moving, companies with the dynamic capability to sense changes in their external environment beyond the traditional boundaries of their industry are finding innovative ways to seize profitable sustainability-related business opportunities. By cooperating with a wide range of stakeholders, the leaders of these organizations are able to sense the challenges of the changing dynamics through partnership with others outside their organizations. Such partnerships allow them to develop the best and most innovative solutions, ones that are both profitable and good for this world.

Certainly one sector that at times has been slow moving is U.S. auto production. Yet in an interview at the Wisdom 2.0 conference in August of 2013, about the leadership courage it takes to sense new dynamics, Bill Ford talked openly about gridlock and pointed to the creativity and cooperation it will take to avoid four billion cars with no place to go. As he says, "even if all the cars are clean, a clean traffic jam is still a traffic jam. . . . It's a human rights issue if you can't move food and healthcare in urban areas." Ford's willingness to talk about such issues has led to a new sense of purpose: "I now refer to Ford as a mobility company rather than a car and truck company. . . . There is a recognition in the company . . . a sense of energy around it."

Creating value for stakeholders requires a business model deliberately designed to include mutually reinforcing interdependencies among the stakeholders. Whole Foods has articulated such a business model. Southwest Airlines has also designed and delivered one. When executed effectively, such business approaches have the potential to far exceed the performance of traditional business models. In today's world no company or organization can have all the knowledge, ideas, and capabilities needed to win. Only by effectively engaging externally can an organization identify, leverage, and co-create the best and most appropriate resources and capabilities. It takes aware leadership and gifted teams to do so.

It is evident that sustainability megatrends will continue to create business risks and opportunities in every sector of the economy, but even the best response built on the business case is failing to produce business vibrancy or a path to a flourishing society.

Paradoxically, profit opportunities are most likely to be realized by business leaders who are authentically motivated to contribute to a flourishing world rather than interested only in achieving competitive advantage. Stakeholders of all kinds, particularly employees, are hungry for leadership that shows genuine and powerful motivation beyond narrow self-interest based on economic calculus alone.

Evidence suggests that there is a growing desire in individuals at all levels of organizations to find greater meaning and to lead lives of service to others that will lead to better prospects for future generations. This trend toward a wider search for meaning and a richer definition of the good life and its legacy is the dimension we turn to next.

Internal Motives Driving People's Increased Desire for Meaning

We continue to reflect on Patricia Aburdene's words, that the focus on spirituality in business is becoming so pervasive that it stands as "today's greatest megatrend." Though some might be taken aback by what seems to be hyperbole on her part, she is still pointing us in an important direction by arguing that more and more people are making choices in the marketplace as "values-driven consumers"—an observation echoed by Harvard University professor Lynn S. Paine in her book *Value Shift*.[24] Aburdene further observes that the power of spirituality is increasingly impacting our personal lives and is spreading into organizations in a way that has the potential to foster transformation in them—if we will let it. We hear people say openly, and proudly, "I'm voting with my dollars. I'm creating the world I want by where I spend my money." That's a new conversation.

Harvard philosopher Michael Sandel, in his recent book, *What Money Can't Buy: The Moral Limits of Markets*, talks about drifting "from having a market economy to becoming a market society. A market economy is a tool—a valuable and effective tool—for organizing productive activity. But a market society is a place where everything is up for sale. It is a way of life where market values govern every sphere of life." As a result, civic practices are disappearing, and people mourn their loss. As every aspect of existence becomes increasingly commercialized, we end up with what Sandel calls the "skyboxification of American life." This state of affairs is leaving many people uneasy and longing for something more.

Offering a somewhat more "far out" perspective, Oxford-trained physicist and author Jude Currivan sees a collective change of consciousness among people, as a growing phenomenon worldwide.[25] In an observation that will resonate for some and make others uneasy, she says, "The veil between worlds is getting thinner, our collective unconscious is awakening, we're beginning to communicate with many other realms of existence and we're remembering the ultimate oneness of ourselves and the entirety of the Cosmos."[26]

Using the Spiral Dynamics of Don Beck and Christopher Cowan to discern different levels of awareness,[27] Currivan links the new vision of a global village to the corresponding evolution of our consciousness. Only in what Beck characterizes as the eighth and final stage of development (which he calls a vMeme, for values-attracting meme) are we able to perceive fully the interconnected whole-world reality. Currivan believes that it is only through such a change in consciousness that we will ultimately succeed in changing the human condition for the better.

But interconnectedness has many meanings these days. We live in a hyperconnected world, as Thomas Friedman and Michael Mandelbaum remind us[28]—a world that is a reflection of globalization and social media trends. Yet we experience a sense of disconnect from what is meaningful—a disconnect from other people and the natural world. We are beginning to recognize the connectedness of things, but in a way that makes us fearful, such as in news of extreme weather events, stories of financial collapse, cases of competition for limited resources, and the possibility of pandemics. In these cases, connection is breeding fear rather than fostering innovations that create possibilities and positive meaning.

Seeing the world as deeply interconnected is a perspective shared by many of the world's major spiritual traditions. It is also a perspective shared by thought leaders in the fields of sustainability and business management: more than a third of the people we interviewed defined *spirituality* as interconnectedness or as being part of a larger whole. Here are two examples of what we heard:

Spirituality is an important dimension of experience where we experience the miracle of life on this planet. . . . [It] includes feelings of intimate interdependence—how everything is part and parcel of everything else—and how the world appears mysterious and beyond our understanding.

Spirituality recognizes that we are part of a living universe and that we are trying to reconnect with the natural world from which we come.

Our interviews with sustainability thought leaders pointed to a deep and growing desire for meaning and connectedness that they see spreading within the business community. Both our secondary research (scanning published research in the field) and our conversations with interview participants reaffirmed the hunger for spirituality in the business realm. Many of our interviewees suggested that spirituality could deepen sustainability by helping organizations become more aware of interconnectedness and by helping people "bring their whole selves to work"—in other words, helping them to be more authentic.

During the years ahead, which many believe will be a period of increasing and challenging instability, the greater the number of people who grow spiritually and engage in their work as part of a connected whole, the greater will be the chance that we will not only survive alongside other species but thrive as consciously thinking and feeling beings.

CHAPTER 3

The Roots of Flourishing

Sustainability framed primarily in terms of meeting material needs is leading us at best to a mode of surviving rather than thriving. In addition, almost everything being done in the name of sustainability has been designed to reduce negative impacts rather than contribute to a healthy world. If our enterprises are to help lead the way toward the far more desirable and fulfilling goal of prosperity and flourishing, they will need more than the usual business case for sustainability. They will need a new spirit—one able to provide a critical boost of energy, creativity, and staying power aimed at the flourishing of the individual, the organization, and the global systems of which they are a part.

To get to prosperity and flourishing, we will need to go beyond our usual language and thinking. We will need to tap into the power of human emotions and motivations grounded in caring and con-nection. The path to engaging this entirely more powerful set of understandings and motivations connects our earlier exploration of sustainability to the transformative power of reflective practices. That path and the research behind it are rooted in both science and spirituality—including recent scientific findings that are increasing our respect for the power of the ethereal realm that we term *spirituality*.

While the spiritual realm can be seen as an individual's orienta-tion toward a deep sense of caring—as we said earlier, a caring for self, for others, and for the world—it can also be expressed in very practical terms. We're reminded of the story of a new middle school built in the midst of a muddy Iowa field whose students came back into the building after a rain-drenched fire drill. The principal was at the back of the crowd, which was moving way too slowly. Standing in the rain, soaking wet, she couldn't figure out the reason for the slow-down. Then she got to the door, and saw hundreds of pairs of muddy shoes neatly lining the hallway. Like anyone who knows the messy habits of middle schoolers, she was astonished at the sight—until she remembered the three rules the school lived by: *Take care of yourself. Take care of each other. Take care of this place.* The kids' care was evident. They were living the values for which so many of us are long-ing. Yet we can see all around us the lack of care—in signs as varied as hyperconsumption ("shop till you drop"), the growing inequality of income between rich and poor individuals as well as between rich and poor countries, and the unmet costs of more frequent extreme weather events worsened by our inattention to environmental dam-age. In business we see it in the sadly self-serving decisions that some managers make at the expense of others. We can spot it in the deci-sions that often rise to the level of headlines "above the fold" in news-papers across the nation, as in 2007–2008, when investment bankers lined their pockets by making huge bets on the U.S. housing crash.

How do we restore and reconnect with our individual and collec-tive ability to care? How can we strengthen our capacity for making decisions that naturally and habitually support the well-being of all? An essential step forward is to invest time and attention in reflective practices that help us to regain a consciousness of connectedness, keeping in mind that it is only when we have a such a sense of con-nectedness—to our life's purpose (or calling), to other people, and to all life—that we reacquire and strengthen our capacity to think and act in ways that support flourishing.

Exploring the Roots

We now turn to the following central questions.

1. Why should spiritual experience, fostered by a variety of reflec-tive practices such as meditation and nature immersion, lead to a greater sense of connectedness?

2. How does a greater sense of connectedness lead to caring for self and others?

3. When does caring lead to taking action that supports flourishing at every scale?

The research presented in this chapter takes you "behind the scenes" with emerging evidence of the transformative role that reflective practices can play in shaping how we think and act.

Of course for some readers, no evidence of transformation is needed. Instead, all they need is faith that God will lead them to that sense of connection and care. Yet even for those who act from faith, the insights presented here may help make sense of emerging scientific discoveries as well as ancient spiritual traditions that affirm the importance of spiritual practices in determining how we relate to, and act in, the material world. These insights may also help those who have faith to feel grounded enough to stand up more often, and more readily, for their spiritual principles in their business environment.

Part of the "behind the scenes" work has to do with the nature of beliefs and how they shape our thinking and behaviors. Seeing how our beliefs impact our actions in the world makes clear the role of specific reflective practices in transforming those beliefs. As beliefs are transformed, new habits of thought and action are created, including those that support flourishing.

We want to emphasize that key dimensions of organizational culture must eventually align with the goal of flourishing if individual reflective practices are to contribute to organizational transformation. Attention to organizational culture is important because when individual efforts are embedded in an organization's culture, individual transformation has the potential to create lasting change in the business—but *only* the potential. Business cultures, like the culture of any institution—from family to nation—are often slow to change. So although reflective processes support the flourishing of individuals, those flourishing individuals must then attend to transforming the organizational structures and processes that are necessary to their organization's ongoing pursuit of flourishing. The reshaped processes and structures will need to be held in place, solidified, by persistent personal and collective determination, fostered by reflective practices, if organizational change is to last over time.

Despite the commonly held notion that culture resists change, most of us can also bring to mind counterexamples in organizations, teams, communities, and even families; instances when a sudden shift in framing, or thinking, catches on and a "sea change" results, producing a permanent change in our of way of operating, such as recycling or turning off the lights when leaving the building. Malcolm Gladwell's popular *Tipping Point*[1] alerted our culture to those instances in which permanent change can take hold surprisingly fast.[2] It is these tipping-point opportunities that we are looking for and that give fresh encouragement to each of us to act on behalf of huge and pressing global challenges.

The Beliefs That Shape our Thinking and Behavior

If reflective practice can help us shift our beliefs and if it is that shift that opens the possibility of creating the world we yearn for, then we need to be able to alter those beliefs when needed. To do that, we need to understand *what* beliefs are, *how* they function, and *where* they come from. The most useful beliefs to work with here, given our pursuit, are those that shape our current thinking and behaviors about sustainability, including those inherited from a time before human-induced threats to our crowded planet existed.

American pragmatist Charles S. Pierce defined *belief* as that upon which one is willing to act. "The essence of belief is the establishment of a habit, and different beliefs are distinguished by the different modes of action to which they give rise."[3] Belief is similar to what management thought leader Peter Senge calls our mental models, those "deeply held internal images of how the world works, images that limit us to familiar ways of thinking and acting."[4] Mental models offer a certain operational efficiency by creating a mental shorthand for how to think about things. Beliefs are also related to the notion of a paradigm, a scientific worldview that shifts from time to time in a tectonic wrench of thinking, which Thomas Kuhn sketched for us in his history of scientific revolutions.[5] Senge reminds us that it is critical to check in regularly to identify those beliefs that may no longer serve us well and need to be replaced with ones that can be more effective in a changing context.

Minnesota poet Robert Bly, famous for his quick wit, says that each of us has a three-thousand-year-old child in our head, giving us antiquated advice like "eat only elk" and "avoid elevators." Bly's last lines about that child?[6]

> . . . He's got six big ideas.
> Five don't work. Right now he's repeating them to you.

What are the ideas in our head that once made sense and which, though now senseless and perhaps even dangerous, we keep repeating to ourselves?

John Ehrenfeld reminds us about the dangerous power of outmoded ideas specifically in the context of sustainability. "Our everyday objective way of holding reality is one of our root causes of unsustainability," he writes. "[For example] the idea of the separation of the mind from the world supports the idea of human mastery over nature, as we see ourselves as outside rather than as a part of the natural world."[7]

If beliefs influence the way we think and act, then what leads us to hold the ones we have? What allows us to change our beliefs to increase our capacity to think and act in support of flourishing? How can we be aware of the limitations of current beliefs and willingly explore a new viewpoint with a greater consciousness of connectedness?

Reflective practices are powerful means to raise our awareness of our current beliefs, helping us to see *what* we see and *why* we see it. That awareness opens us to experience greater connectedness across different points of view, and gives us a willingness to shift to a new set of beliefs that favor thinking and acting that are consistent with flourishing.

We see this process of achieving greater awareness of our mindsets and thought processes in *Presence* (by Peter Senge, Otto Scharmer, Joseph Jaworski, and Betty Sue Flowers),[8] a precursor to Otto Scharmer's *Theory U*.[9] Scharmer outlines reflective practices for opening our minds—a process that, although not spiritual in origin, results in what its practitioners characterize as *open heart* and *open will*—leading to an orientation that is certainly spiritual in tone and feel. Awareness of spiritual experience, and being comfortable with that dimension of human experience, becomes an important capacity of management in any organization that wants to place sustainability at the heart of the enterprise in a way that will be lasting and meaningful.

We can understand the role and power of beliefs more easily by grouping them into two categories: what we call *Level 1* beliefs and *Level 2* beliefs. Level 1 beliefs tell us something about the meaning people give to everyday life. They shed light on such questions as what we take to be human nature, what the purpose of business is, and what our relationship is to the earth. At Level 1 we are still conscious of the questions and of our answers, at least to some degree. But Level 2 beliefs lie outside our awareness. They rest within our often hidden assumptions about the nature of reality and they tend to condition or shape our Level 1 beliefs without our necessarily knowing it.

The distinction between Level 1 and a Level 2 can help the curious reader make sense of the hierarchy of beliefs that moves us progressively toward the underlying bedrock of ideas we hold about humans as separate (or connected) and selfish (or caring). Understanding why we act the way we do is essential to our capacity to shift our ways of acting away from unsustainability and toward flourishing, which is our overall intent.

So now let's play with the power of these two levels by beginning to trace a business-oriented set of current and emerging beliefs.

LEVEL I BELIEFS

The beliefs that have been dominant since the Industrial Revolution embrace the economic assumption that humans are self-interested utility maximizers.[10] They include the *enterprise belief* that the sole purpose of business is profit and competitive advantage; the *societal belief* that the main goal for humankind is economic growth and technological progress; and the *environmental belief* that nature's resources exist above all for human consumption. This interlocking set of ideas creates a strong, sometimes seemingly unassailable structure of thought, like a fish in water, swimming in the only world it's ever known and feeling at ease in its element. In much the same way, our ideas built on the scaffolding of Level 1 beliefs have come to be seen as perfectly normal and unassailable.

In this intertwining set of beliefs, being rich is defined not by who we are, that is, by who we are *being,* but by what we *have.*[11] Wealth is measured not by the quality of our life experience but by the quantity of goods we own. All that may seem obvious, even normal, to us. "Greed is good" is Gordon Gekko's famous line in Oliver Stone's 1987 film *Wall Street.* Author Don Mayer cites several aspects of consumerism that dominate U.S. culture, including that "nations and corporations must grow in order to 'progress,' that nature is no more than a storehouse of resources, that spirituality has no place in business, and that rational individuals will strive to amass as much material wealth . . . as possible."[12] For further evidence of a culture of consumerism, he points to the 1995 book *God Wants You to Be Rich.*[13]

The limitations and unintended consequences of these interlocking beliefs—our legacy inherited from an earlier time—are becoming evident. Individuals experience hopelessness and despair—an unshakable questioning of "is this all there is," a sense of having climbed the wrong mountain, or having climbed a ladder that was leaning against the wrong wall. Businesses are trapped in an endless cycle of outperforming each other and trying to meet ever higher analyst expectations, a process that exhausts and distracts the leadership and leaves the workforce in a constant state of anxiety. Developed and developing countries alike are questioning whether economic growth is producing the quality of life that their citizens want, let alone one they can sustain. The earth itself is reaching critical thresholds, in terms of climate, water, top soil, and other natural systems, beyond which its ability to support life as we know it is at risk. It is becoming apparent that as long as we operate from our outmoded beliefs, we can no longer hope to bring about true sustainability or the quality of life for which increasing numbers of us yearn.

At the same time as this legacy of interlocking ideas, this older set of beliefs, seems to have us in its grip, we can nonetheless discern *emerging* beliefs that are quite different from the legacy notions and wholly consistent with the pursuit of flourishing. Many of these beliefs are held by young people, who seem to look at our choices with some puzzlement. One such emerging belief, especially among the younger generation, is that a sense of complete well-being is more important than material success alone. A second emerging belief is that to care for others is an essential quality of what it means to be human. A growing number of people would think it strange that in our teams we fret that someone isn't pulling their weight because they are caring for their sick child or an ailing parent. A third such belief is that cooperation is a powerful basis for business success. But as we live with our older beliefs about the harsh world of competition, we begin to worry that in our workplace we'll be taken advantage of if we come across as supportive of others. We'll be seen as too soft. A fourth emerging belief is that happiness is a more desirable societal goal and measure than gross national product. We mull this one over in table conversations, finally telling ourselves and each other that it cannot be changed.[14] And finally, there is the acknowledgement that the earth is a fragile, exhaustible, living system entrusted to our care. Shrugging our shoulders we say, "But what can we do?" So we are taken aback when a "young-un" gently suggests that we are wasting our lives and spoiling the earth by our obsession with material wealth. In this alternative set of nested beliefs that are emerging among a growing number of people around the world, a commitment to flourishing is an obvious choice.

These emerging beliefs have important implications for corporate sustainability efforts aimed at creating value for society and nature in ways that create even more value for customers and shareholders. One implication is that such corporate efforts need to pay more attention to the *flourishing of individuals,* which also requires a change in thinking. We noted earlier that personal flourishing has been largely ignored by management theory over the past century. Economics and business strategy have tended to treat individuals as no more than efficient cogs in a machine (which coincidentally is how unhappy employees say they feel in their workplace) or as transactionable inputs who seek only to maximize material rewards. Yet without flourishing individuals and the energy, commitment, ingenuity, and creativity they bring, we cannot expect flourishing at the scale of business and society. In a recent survey reported in the *Wall Street Journal,* an astonishing 52 percent of all full-time workers in America said they were unenthusiastic about their work, and an additional 18 percent said they were disconnected to the point of interfering with their colleagues' ability to perform.[15] The loss in creativity and productivity of such disengagement is staggering.

In Figure 3.1, the goal of economic growth and technological progress is replaced with the broader goal of prosperity and flourishing, which implies healthy whole systems at every level, from the individual to the biosphere. Clearly a set of beliefs aimed at creating a flourishing world does not hold nature as a bank of resources and services to be exploited and spent down no matter what the consequences. In such a world, business contributes more than traditional economic value to its customers and owners. It creates *sustainable value,*[16] by "doing good" for society and nature in ways that allow the enterprise to do even better economically.

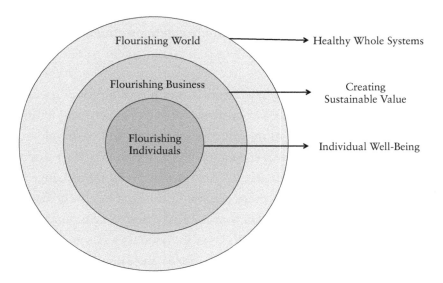

FIGURE 3.1   Flourishing at Every Scale

Such a thriving business in service of a healthy world understands that individuals are more than self-interested utility maximizers and treats them accordingly. The task of management encompasses caring for the well-being of individuals, whether they are employees, customers, suppliers, or external business partners. To see someone as a flourishing individual, we must assume that the person has integrity of being, that their emotional and spiritual health must be taken into account along with their material reward and physical comfort. The people who are part of a business become transformed, in everyone's thinking, from mere economic production functions to real, living individuals with the full resources they bring with them to work. Because our places of work play such an important role in all our lives, for the good of the firm and the good of the person, business organizations must serve the whole human being and not just the economic part of each person.

Although extensive research has been conducted on the relationship between business and society, a clear vision of the role of the individual in embedding sustainability has not been fleshed out. Yet it is the role played by the individual that may be the essential factor in speeding the evolution of our responses to global and local sustainability challenges, for the sake of business, society as a whole, and indeed the planet. In the emerging set of beliefs that includes the flourishing of individuals, sustainability goals are reformulated as follows:

Flourishing world: Societies that are economically, socially, culturally, and politically thriving as well as resilient. A natural environment comprising healthy systems, whether at the level of local forest ecology, the oceans, or the earth itself. A world in which other species coexist with humans and thrive in their own milieu.

Flourishing business: Organizations that generate sustainable value by creating value synergistically for shareholders and stakeholders. Engaged teams and high-performance groups operating in a culture of effectiveness *and* living the personal values of their members. By creating value for society and nature, they find ways to create even more value for their customers and investors.

Flourishing individuals: Individuals who are full of vitality, for whom the "spirit within" is awakened, who are deeply in touch with their own purpose, and who feel connected to others, to community, and to all life on the earth. For such individuals, *being* becomes increasingly more important than *having,* and caring becomes an intrinsic quality of their way of being.

Exactly what happens when we apply these two differing belief sets—the legacy beliefs from earlier times and the emergent beliefs— to a specific illustration in today's world of work? By looking at how each set of beliefs influences business purpose and strategy, we can see the contrast in outcomes that such differing beliefs produce. We can then choose which outcomes to pursue.

COMPETITIVE ADVANTAGE VERSUS COOPERATIVE ADVANTAGE

If you ask five executives the purpose of their business strategy, at least four will say it is to create competitive advantage and shareholder value.[17] This is the shared "common sense," the dominant paradigm in business today, which has been taught in business schools since the early 1980s, when Michael Porter published his groundbreaking books *Competitive Strategy* and *Competitive Advantage*. It became further entrenched in our thinking in the 1990s with the rise of the Economic Value Added (EVA) techniques developed by Stern Stewart & Co. and the linking of these return-on-economic-capital measures to executive pay. The concepts of competitive advantage and shareholder value are now so intertwined and engrained in how we do business that most top management teams, as busy and pressured as they are, do not question their legitimacy or their usefulness. Not unlike the indigenous people of America who tried to hold off the first British cannons with bows and arrows, they have neither the energy nor the inclination to go back to basics in their thinking. Yet these indigenous cultures could not win the war with old thinking. Despite thousands of books on strategic management, countless MBA programs, and hundreds of management consulting firms, very few businesses remain highly successful beyond more than a single generation of consumers. Once their environment, industry structure, or dominant business model changes, they are no longer nearly as successful. You might wonder to what extent their certainty, their habitual way of thinking, blocks their learning as conditions change. Take Wang, Blockbuster, Kodak, Barnes & Noble, Xerox, AT&T, and even IBM. All of these companies either lost their way permanently or needed a turnaround artist such as Lou Gerstner to get them back on top. The constant shift in companies that populate the Fortune Global 500, 10 percent of which exit each year, is a stark indicator of the limitations in one of the dominant paradigms of management. There seems to be a wake-up call in all of this.

From the investor perspective, despite a huge increase in executive salaries over the past twenty years, the chase for competitive advantage and shareholder value has not generally translated into superior returns. The correlation between executive pay and performance has been erratic at best. There have been dramatic cases of companies and their leaders using sophisticated techniques to manage accounting earning streams but not actually putting anywhere near the stated financial value into the pockets of the shareholders. At times, such as during the financial crisis of 2008–2009, the wrongheadedness of such techniques has resulted in significant unintended consequences for both investors and society at large.

The failure of the legacy paradigm of competitive advantage as the only strategy is not surprising when you consider that competitive advantage is based on the following idealized beliefs about firms, markets, and pricing grounded in industrial economics (and later in neoclassical economics):

1. *Firms* are homogeneous production functions.

2. *Markets* are efficient, complete, and faceless, in equilibrium with rational players; all assets are tradable and there is no cost to technology transfer.

3. *Pricing* information is transparent, assets are fully priced, and prices reflect all opportunities.

Practically none of these beliefs reflect the actual, complex world faced by business leaders today. Remember Robert Bly's notion of six big ideas, five of them wrong, that your inner voice is repeating to you right now?

In contrast to the idea of rational markets, the financial and business world of today is messy and faces a number of large and poorly understood risks. Firms are less and less homogeneous than they used to be. Behavioral economists such as Daniel Kahneman have shown that many social and emotional factors influence economic decision-making. The inability of the smartest financial minds to appreciate and understand the true scope of interconnection, interrelationships, irrationality, and risks across the global financial market is one example of how different today's world is from the world of the abstract beliefs of early economic theory.

The concept of *cooperative advantage* recognizes that the unsustainabilities we face in just about every sector pose radically new business opportunities for which cooperative innovation is a key success factor. It also recognizes that in today's complex, dynamic, and interdependent world, value creation requires attracting and effectively cooperating with the best partners in order to sense and shape the external environment, source and seize innovative opportunities, and adapt to changing conditions. To understand the strategic value that cooperative advantage can provide to business, it is helpful to consider strategy in a way quite different from the legacy framework. This concept of strategy includes four interrelated dimensions: the operational environment, strategic priorities, the capabilities required for strategic success, and the stakeholders on which the enterprise depends. In whatever way strategic priorities are established, one must ask what roles internal and external cooperation play with respect to each of these dimensions. In every case, one has to ask whether improved cooperation among employees and external stakeholders could help the enterprise deliver on these priorities. The emerging framework of cooperation and collaboration creates different and more powerful questions for leadership.

The logic for creating strategic value from superior cooperation that underlies the idea of cooperative advantage is derived from well-established and highly researched theories of strategic management, including resource dependence, the resource-based view of the firm, dynamic capabilities, and stakeholder theory. These theories consider the complexities of today's real-world firms, which are diverse organizations with unique bundles of capabilities and embedded in networks of interdependencies and social relationships. In this world, and from this viewpoint, markets may be inefficient, incomplete, and in disequilibrium. In this world, relationships matter and players often do not behave rationally. We see that some assets get built and many of the most important ones, such as know-how and goodwill, either cannot be traded or have high transfer costs. This is a world where pricing is often opaque and assets are often not priced at their strategic value.

When this world is seen through the lens of the emergent paradigm of cooperative advantage, it seems evident that considerable unexploited opportunity exists to create value for both business and society. But that value will be realized only by managers who have the mindset and associated skills that allow them to see it. Mindset is like a road that leads us unavoidably in a certain direction. As the saying goes, if you're going in the wrong direction, it's never too soon to turn around.

We know from the work of Peter Senge and many others that the beliefs we hold greatly influence the way we think and act in business. Yet to understand *why* we hold our Level 1 beliefs, we have to dig deeper into our assumptions about the nature of reality itself. These deeper assumptions offer each of us a starting point for considering our own deeply held, and often partially obscured, beliefs about the nature of reality. They allow for other ways to represent accurately what we consider to be how the world works. They enable us to work more effectively with people who have a different perspective on how the world works.

LEVEL 2 BELIEFS

Level 2 beliefs—our deeper assumptions about the nature of reality— shape the everyday (Level 1) beliefs on which we base our thinking and acting. The way we think and act is in turn vital to our goal of meaningfully and persistently embedding sustainability-as-flourishing. So digging around in these deeper assumptions can hit real pay dirt. Though it might be tempting to jump into action by going straight to the practices described in later chapters, we invite you to try your hand at the "shovel work" required to unearth these deeper assumptions.

That work will open the possibility of understanding more completely the roots of *un*sustainability and why changing minds and hearts, particularly in our businesses, is so crucial and can be so difficult. Such an inquiry will also have the practical value of alerting you to the deeper assumptions at work within you and around you.

It helps our exposition of ideas to group Level 2 beliefs into three subcategories, reflecting their source: science, faith, and social constructionism. Scientific beliefs are those that emerge from scientific experimentation and theorizing. Those based on experimentation are held to be more firmly established than those based on theory alone. Scientific beliefs or truths are said to mirror an objective world that exists outside our minds. Faith-based beliefs or truths are based on the authority of an individual or an institution such as a religion and do not require further evidence. They cannot be verified by experimentation because they refer to nonworldly phenomena; if they could be verified, they would become science-based.

Our third category, social constructionism, begins from an entirely different premise about how we make meaning of reality. It considers the meaning we make of our world to be the consequence of the language we use to describe and interact with the world.[18] Along this vein, Gregory Bateson says, "The major problems in the world are the result of the difference between how nature works and the way people think."[19] This is an insight essential to understanding the systems practices provided in Chapter 7.

In summary, science and faith believe that objective reality is there to be discovered, although the means differ in each case, whereas social constructionists believe that the meaning we give to reality is subjectively created through language and our interaction with the world. Let's see, then, how we can sharpen and broaden our understanding of Level 2 beliefs by exploring their sources and the changes that are occurring within each source.

Science. Current dominant beliefs about the physical world have come in part from science as it has advanced over the past 2,500 years and particularly over the three hundred years since the Age of Enlightenment.[20] For example, we are taught that all matter is made up of particles (atoms, protons, neutrons, electrons, and now additional subatomic particles) that tend to clump together as discrete objects in space. In classical physics, these objects are subject to the gravitational and electromagnetic fields, and at the subatomic scale, to the strong and weak nuclear fields. Until recently, these four fields were assumed to be the only forces or "actions at a distance" that condition the behavior of an object in space.

Emerging science, sometimes referred to as the "new sciences,"— not yet dominant but a subcurrent of scientific thinking that is working its way to the surface (like a theme in a symphony just becoming audible)—has come across intriguing phenomena that cannot be explained without supposing the existence of an interconnecting field that underlies the physical world as we know it. Quantum physics has gathered well-established evidence for such a fifth field, known as the Yang-Mills field, according to which the smallest known particles are not thought of as "little billiard balls" but rather as field "excitations" that look like particles.

In other words, the physical world of our grandparents was made up of particles and fields (such as the gravitational field), but in quantum theory, the physical world is made up only of fields. All matter is seen as excited states of a field. Similar evidence exists for the connectedness of living systems, such as the human body or the biosphere. Instead of depending on chance mutations in the genome, evolution is now seen as a finely tuned process with an extraordinarily high level of coherence between species and their environments.[21]

This expansion of scientific thought has had huge and immediate consequences for how we see the world around us: instead of thinking of ourselves as separate and discreet from one another and from nature, the new sciences suggest that we are all part of one interconnected fabric. In the language of quantum physics, instead of consisting of corpuscular particles, we are vibrational patterns of space-time.

Faith. A parallel set of dominant Level 2 beliefs can be found in a wide range of religious traditions. According to Lynn White Jr., in his classic 1967 article on the roots of our ecological crisis, Christian anthropocentrism led us to believe "we are superior to nature, contemptuous of it, and willing to use it for our slightest whim."[22] God created the world as we know it, but when man named all the animals, he established his dominance over them. Man is not part of nature; he is made in God's image. An alternative Christian view, famously articulated by Francis of Assisi in the thirteenth century, is enjoying a revival: it sees all creatures as enjoying equality with man. This view reminds us that our stewardship of creation is a central though often overlooked theme in Genesis. Along these lines, Mary Evelyn Tucker and John Grim led a research project that shows how development across many religions is "contributing to the emergence of a broader cosmological orientation and environmental ethics based on diverse sensibilities of the sacred dimensions of the more-than-human world."[23] For the last twenty years of his life, White himself urged his fellow Christians to move beyond not just the biblical notion of dominion but also an ethic of stewardship to what he referred to as a "third legitimately Biblical position" in which humans might begin to think and act as if we are members of what has been called a "spiritual democracy of all God's creatures.[24]"

Variants of these beliefs advanced by both science and religion can also be found in philosophy and in spiritual traditions. We are rediscovering the ancient wisdom of Greek philosophers and spiritual leaders as well as that of eastern sages and mystics from the three Abrahamic religions—Christianity, Islam, and Judaism[25]—who espouse that there is a deeper, hidden dimension to the physical world. For Pythagoras it was the Kosmos, the background of form and matter from which all being in the world arises. Pythagoras conceived of the universe as a vast lyre in which each planet, vibrating at a specific pitch, harmonized with other heavenly bodies to create a "music of the spheres," an idea that William Shakespeare recast in his play *The Merchant of Venice.*[26] The term *cosmos,* as coined by Pythagoras, is similar to the Zoroastrian term *aša,* which refers to the concept of a divine order, or divinely ordered creation. Plato believed in an eternal realm of Ideas and Forms; for Plotinus, the hidden dimension was a supreme transcendent "One" containing no division and beyond all categories of being and nonbeing. For the Vedantic scholars of ancient India, it was the Brahman, the one supreme reality that is the origin of the phenomenal universe from which all manifest reality arises. Another term, used synonymously with Brahman in the Upanishads, is *Akasha,* about which Swami Vivekananda said the following:

It is the omnipresent, all-penetrating existence. Everything that has form, everything that is the result of combination, is evolved out of this Akasha. It is Akasha that becomes the air, that becomes the liquids, that becomes the solids; it is the Akasha that becomes the sun, the earth, the moon, the stars, the comets; it is the Akasha that becomes the human body, the animal body, the plants, every form that we see, everything that can be sensed, everything that exists. It cannot be perceived; it is so subtle that it is beyond all ordinary perception; it can only be seen when it has become gross, has taken form.[27]

Thus modern science, religion, philosophy, and perennial intuitions about the nature of reality are converging on an interconnected "source of everything" that gives order to the world. Yet in spite of this convergence among thought leaders, from scientists to spiritual leaders, as a species we are slow to catch on to the new way of thinking. The following anecdote is an amusing illustration of this inertia in our collective thinking: In the early 1990s the *New York Times* reported that the Vatican had issued a statement that Galileo (who had been part of the "new" science three hundred years earlier) was right after all. In his case, it took only three hundred years for the acknowledgment to be made.

Social constructionism. Science is a method for producing beliefs about the world. It is the best way we have found to gain knowledge about the way the world works. But it provides no meaning to accompany that knowledge, and without meaning we cannot act in intentional ways. Faith-based beliefs do carry meaning and indeed have provided us with some of the most important guides for human action we have. But for some people they are incomplete and leave us without rules to guide much of everyday life.

Our societies have filled in the gaps with rules we have created through our use of language about the meaning of objects in the world,[28] and about the "right" ways to act with and upon those objects. Our way of understanding reality comes from all three sources (science, faith, and language-based rules), and it is their combination that leads to challenges and confrontation in the course of everyday life, particularly in our organizations. Coming to an understanding that some of our beliefs are neither faith-based nor scientifically derived allows for dialogue and learning, essential characteristics of reflective practices. It places us firmly in the realm of social constructionist thought.

From a social constructionist perspective, our deepest beliefs may be formed in our earliest relationships and interactions, in particular in how we experience love, which Chilean biologist Humberto Maturana defines as "the domain of behaviors through which another arises as a legitimate other in coexistence with oneself."[29] According to Maturana, love is the essential ingredient for language to exist, and there is language only if there is intimacy. The lack of separateness and the absence of words that we experience at the beginning of our life may be one of the few moments when we experience the essence of love. We hold that understanding of reality until we begin to name our experiences and make sense of them. That act of naming creates separation.

Among all emotions, love is the foundation of our sociability.[30] The basis of language and its emotional origin are to be found in the intimacy of mutual admiration and care, having developed in the network of "matristic" relationships that constitute interactions in the early moments of human sociability.

Awareness of connectedness is therefore part of our earliest experiences. We would argue that it appears earlier than our first sense of separation. We are born with the confidence that we are loved and accepted, and with an implicit trust. It is only in our social interactions, as we grow older, that we transform love into a kind of transaction in which we give an emotion to another rather than experience the "we" of shared humanity.

The Role of Reflective Practices

We have been using the term *reflective practices* as an umbrella term to include those practices often associated with spirituality (for example, some forms of meditation) as well as other practices that are not necessarily related to spiritual practice (for example, the creative arts, music, and journal writing). Such practices, whether spiritual or nonspiritual in origin, allow us to "still the mind" and access our deeper wisdom.

Seventeenth-century philosopher and mathematician Blaise Pascal, in his now classic *Pensées,* famously said, "All of humanity's problems stem from man's inability to sit quietly in a room alone." His point was that our busyness is a form of distraction that we choose in order to avoid facing the realities of our existence. Reflective practices help stop the frenetic distractions of everyday life and enable us to become more aware of what is important to us. Without such practices, as Pascal suggests, distractions lead us to hide our heads in the sand, leaving us blind to the unintentional consequences of our actions for others and for the world.

Reflective practices also strengthen our understanding of connection. They do so by enabling a more authentic and deeply human way of being in the world.[31] If caring is inherent in what it means to be human, then reflective practices are a way to rediscover our humanity. While some reflective practices suggest emptying the mind, others, such as mindfulness meditation, ask that we simply practice being present to thoughts and feelings, sitting with them (literally, in this "sitting practice") and establishing an increasingly calm equanimity and presence to what the world offers us. The value of the practice is that it strengthens the individual's awareness of his or her thoughts and feelings. It is this awareness, and the attendant ability to choose alternative patterns of thought and feeling, that over time creates a genuine steadiness and centeredness in the face of life's challenges.

In addition, reflective practices may enable us to physically tap into an interconnecting coherence-producing field, allowing us to sense the underlying harmony, elegance, and order of the universe. Neurophysiological evidence already exists for the effects of reflective practices on the brain and nervous system.[32] In a study at Stanford University, researchers found that "even just a few minutes of loving-kindness meditation increased feelings of social connection and positivity,"[33] conferring tangible physical and mental health benefits. Another point of reference comes from research conducted at the University of Texas that underscores the positive health impacts of journal writing.[34]

Evidence also exists that the brain's subneuronal networks process information on the quantum level. In this view,[35] there are two structures in the brain that process the signals we receive from the world: the macro-level neuroaxonal networks, which process information coming from our five senses; and the subneuronal lattice-within-microtubules networks, which process information at the quantum level. Experiments show that reflective experiences, such as meditation, esthetic experience, or the contemplation of nature, synchronize and harmonize the electrical activity of the left and right hemispheres of the brain in a way that is absent during ordinary states of consciousness. The implication is that information we pick up through reflective practice may enable us to grasp an underlying order and harmony of the universe: the Oneness on which a growing number of beliefs are converging.

These insights from multiple scientific disciplines suggest that reflective practices may in fact be acts of "tuning in" to the underlying field from which both matter and consciousness spring. Such a direct positive impact of reflective practices on our physical, mental, and emotional well-being and on our sense of connectedness was reflected in the interviews we had with more than three dozen business and thought leaders. As one person told us:

Spirituality helps draw us out of ourselves to connect with others and with life with more sensitivity and can very much condition every act or intervention that we have. . . . It speaks to a way of seeing and being that opens us to the world and makes us better human beings.

Another way to visualize the impact of spirituality on flourishing is shown in the causal loop diagram in Figure 3.2. Causal loops help us to see elements that increase the presence of something we want.

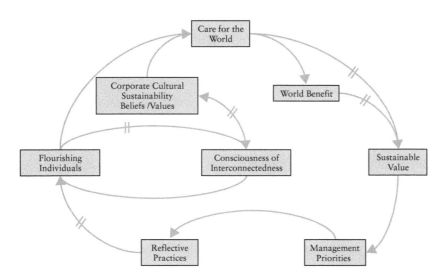

FIGURE 3.2 Causal Loops Starting with Reflective Practices

Such relationships are referred to as "reinforcing loops" and include those that can move us toward flourishing.

The causal loops in Figure 3.2 tell a story of relationships among reflective practices and personal and organizational well-being. They show how reflective practices of the kind we've mentioned can have a positive reinforcing effect (though sometimes with a lag, shown by the double crosslines) on individual well-being by raising a person's awareness of interconnectedness, which in turn contributes further to a sense of flourishing. Flourishing individuals who experience a sense of interconnectedness with others and with the world around them are more likely to exhibit care for the world, and greater creativity. When corporate sustainability beliefs and values are also evident and aligned because of a consciousness of interconnectedness, then the reinforcing impact of individual and organizational awareness of connection has a multiplying effect. Care for the world can lead savvy enterprises to create both world benefit and business value, which in turn improves the chances that management will consider individual, team, and collective reflective practices to be a priority of the enterprise.

Organizational Inertia and Reflective Practices

As individuals develop a stronger sense of connection and caring, their new orientations may not immediately, by themselves, result in things that need to be changed within the organization actually getting changed. Yet reflective practices can influence a dynamic, at first by strengthening the individual's sense of self-knowledge and then by influencing the individual's way of acting in the world. It is the persistence of this new dynamic resulting from reflective practices that can contribute to the disciplined and determined engagement of a critical mass of people who can influence the movement toward prosperity and flourishing.

This process can happen in a variety of ways. While exploring flourishing at every scale, people are likely to learn more about the underlying economic, environmental, health, and social issues that exist at both the local and global levels. They may see that they need to acquire requisite skills and to strengthen their role in creating a high-performing team in order to address those issues. As a result, they may begin to realize that the existing enterprise strategy or culture does not embed sustainability. This may lead to action:

1. They may push for a wiser strategy.

2. They may have to scramble for resources and budget.

3. They may begin to create a broader network of contacts.

4. They may see the need to find new mentors and to acquire the skills to become better leaders.

5. They may begin to see the role of infrastructure and design in supporting the move toward flourishing, and begin working on the design of that infrastructure.

6. They may even leave, seeking an organization that has a strategy or culture oriented toward flourishing.

In our pursuit of flourishing, it is worth keeping in mind an old Eastern spiritual saying about what we should expect from sudden insight or wisdom: "Before enlightenment, chop wood, carry water. After enlightenment, chop wood, carry water." We always have hard work to do. Reflective practices and spiritual experience don't take away the realities of the world and our obligation to deal with them. But they do make this central, foundational difference: they create a greater awareness of interconnectedness and they center each of us in a sense of caring that can increase our persistence and resilience. Persistence and resilience count for a lot in creating organizational cultures aimed at flourishing. For example, we have observed the impact of the Appreciative Inquiry process (described in detail in Chapter 7) on people at all organizational levels. We have watched it create a dynamic in which people seem to transform themselves from feeling helpless about conditions around them into operating as responsible, persistent actors in the life of their organization. Such practices embed persistence and resilience.

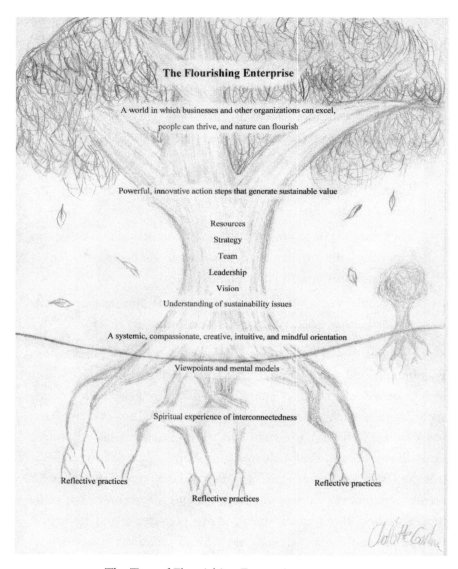

The Flourishing Enterprise

A world in which businesses and other organizations can excel,
people can thrive, and nature can flourish

Powerful, innovative action steps that generate sustainable value

Resources

Strategy

Team

Leadership

Vision

Understanding of sustainability issues

A systemic, compassionate, creative, intuitive, and mindful orientation

Viewpoints and mental models

Spiritual experience of interconnectedness

Reflective practices

Reflective practices

Reflective practices

FIGURE 3.3   The Tree of Flourishing Enterprise
SOURCE: Charlotte Gorham.

Figure 3.3 arrays the different factors required to support a flourishing enterprise. It visually represents the idea that many of the "above the surface" factors—those we usually work on day-to-day in our businesses—depend on what is happening below ground. It is only in the nourishing soil of our beliefs and mental models that transformation can take hold. And it is only (or primarily) through attention to spiritual experience fostered by reflective practices that we can hope to shift those beliefs and mental models enduringly to include the care needed to support flourishing in everything we do.

Although we have made our case for the power of reflective practices in fostering flourishing enterprise, we are all faced with the challenge of working with the inherently slow-to-change nature of organizations. Culture, in business or in any other institution, reflects the structures on which rest the routines that get things done. Unless something shifts in the beliefs and behaviors that are already present, these routines will likely remain entrenched. Because it is these entrenched beliefs and behaviors that need to change, organizational theories aimed at changing or replacing them can help us understand the various other factors that must be wrestled with to enable transformation for flourishing. Of particular value in the move toward flourishing are organizational theories that focus on the power of structures and processes that shift beliefs and behaviors.

We take as a starting point that the reflective practices we share in Chapters 5, 6, and 7 are effective in fostering and supporting transformative change in individuals and in increasing their awareness of the structures and processes that also need transformation. By *transformative change* we mean changes in behavior that persist over reasonably long periods and in a variety of situations—or in the words of a friend who was asked if a setback in life would send him back to the bottle, "Of course not; that's just not who I am anymore." It is that kind of transformative change we are seeking. It is permanently seeing differently, seeing ourselves differently, and therefore naturally acting differently.

We need to care about whether changes in behavior are enduring, particularly within the organizational context. There is good reason to be concerned: the history of organizational change programs is checkered with initiatives that have failed to have lasting impact.

We should also note, however, that many of those change efforts have tended to be rollouts of large-scale work process initiatives and top-down reorganizations rather than the inside-out processes of transformation of thinking and creative insight—the kinds of shifts that we are advocating here and that reflective practices foster.

The practices presented in Chapters 5, 6, and 7 are intended to open people up to new beliefs and norms, at both the individual and group levels within the larger organizational setting. The effectiveness of these practices at allowing the individual and the group to hold onto the change in perspective depends in part on the particular character of the practice, and the disciplined nature of the practitioner. For example, meditative practices can create a sense of peacefulness and caring. Immersion in nature can produce a similar outcome. Dialogue processes aim to develop connectedness and openness among the members of a group. In all cases, the impact of the practices is greater if they are done regularly, one might even say "religiously" (in a nonreligious sense), with attention to the discipline, and without distraction.

How we approach practices within the organization is important, because it's easy to end up in the ditch. We can't sentence people to meditation, as was one executive, who admitted that he'd been "sentenced" to dialogue training because "I mouthed off to my boss." We can't mandate reflection. We can't put reflective practices in the job description and the annual review. The practices need to be supported, encouraged, and wholly voluntary. To be effective in shifting the individual and corporate mindset and values toward flourishing, these individual and group practices must be welcomed rather than imposed or made mandatory. For these practices to be welcomed, people first need to experience some catalyst, personal or organizational, that creates a sense, however subtle, of need for them.

Sometimes the catalysts for change are positive, as in having a clear vision of a future for which people yearn. Other times the initial catalyst for change might be personal pain, or an organizational challenge or obstacle such as stress, high turnover, or simply not getting the wanted results. At still other times the initial catalyst might be a combination of positive and negative motivators. Whichever path in the long run brings people to reflective practice, it is a positive vision of what they want most for their organization and for themselves that has the greatest pulling power. The positive goal, rather than avoidance of a negative outcome, tends to build commitment to the goal, as well as to the practices that lead to the goal. And it is the positive vision, and sustained practice, that can shift the mindset toward a sense of the interconnectedness that vision and practice engender, and toward a habit of caring for all stakeholders.

Fostering such a culture is part of ensuring that individual reflective practices produce the intended outcomes of organizational flourishing. Much wisdom says you can't change culture by going after culture. Instead you go after work. Organization expert Edgar Schein says that when you want a new culture, you give people a difficult new task that can't be accomplished doing things the old way. Then you get out of their way. When you free them to innovate in order to get the work out the door, they thereby build a new culture.[36] Perhaps that's the case for the power of a highly inspiring multigenerational aspirational vision like creating the conditions for humans and all other species to flourish on the earth forever. The power of the work that needs to be done will create the new ways of doing things, which will shape the new culture. We can't get there following our usual practices, constrained by our old culture.

To imagine what effect such spiritually transformed individuals would have on an organization, it helps to have a workable model of organizational behavior. One powerful model has been proposed by sociologist Anthony Giddens.[37] He views organizational culture as a set of permanent or slowly changing routine behaviors that characterize normality or, in the vernacular, what people do every day in the organization. This model has been applied to business organizations to explain how they are shaped by and respond to changes in technologies[38] or in managerial leadership.[39] Giddens' work is based on the premise that you can discern a structure in a culture,[40] a structure shaped in the course of everyday actions. At the same time, that structure conditions normal behavior, producing a reinforcing loop in the systems dynamics sense.[41] Like Schein, Giddens suggests that culture is shaped by the everyday actions of getting the work done. Other models of organizational culture arrive at similar conclusions.

Schein adds another dimension to our understanding of culture, and his insight relates to our earlier exploration of the nature of beliefs. He says that difficulty in changing corporate culture is often due to the hidden structure that lurks below the surface, much like the Level 2 beliefs we discussed earlier. He points out, as have others, that the espoused beliefs and values of an organization are not the ones that actually drive its behavior.[42] Organizations will emphasize the power of data and the importance of truth telling while at the same time some managers keep some data away from others out of fear of losing control or out of worry that messengers bearing bad tidings get shot. These managers may fear that to tell the truth about what they see will turn into a career-limiting move. This is one reason why reflective practices that increase awareness and authenticity—making people more comfortable with speaking their mind and saying what they see—are so effective in addressing the challenges of transforming culture.

Practices that foster dialogue and encourage open democratic inquiry in order to invent new ways to operate are particularly helpful. The much emulated Toyota Production System is grounded in such practices, in which new ways to solve old problems can arise during open inquiry and experimentation.[43] The dialogue work that grew out of MIT under the leadership of physicist David Bohm, and subsequently Peter Senge and his colleagues, instills the practice of balancing open inquiry with speaking a direct point of view or "advocating." It is this balance that allows a group to learn its way through complexity to sustainable action.

Ultimately the beliefs of the organization have to incorporate the new vision of business as an agent of world benefit. In doing so, the organization begins to let go of old beliefs and behaviors that pose obstacles to operating in the new way. This process requires understanding people as complex, multifaceted human beings. In the case of one engineering executive who was struggling to help people let go of an old portion of the business that was clearly losing money, the creative answer was to hold a funeral for the old business. Complete with a coffin, a choir, lavish food, and a celebration at corporate headquarters, the funeral somehow did the necessary work. This very practical executive realized that letting go is hard, and the human difficulty needs to be acknowledge and honored.

Given the stretch between the beliefs driving the old business model and those that reflect the emergent vision of sustainability-as-flourishing, sustained and disciplined reflective practices are needed to shape organizational culture along new and necessary paths. Practices that are effective in opening new beliefs and behaviors at an individual level must come to be evident, practiced by many, and a part of life across the organization in order to have an impact on the organization. What begins as an individual practice of being aware of our thoughts evolves into team practices of sharing those thoughts. Explicit caring behavior within the firm and persistently repeated actions and processes that embody the connectedness of the firm to the world outside are necessary to replace the present, and often unconscious and almost always unexamined, beliefs embedded in the autonomous, always-competitive model of the firm. Moreover, the benefits of these practices will inevitably be challenged by the normal business pressure to answer massive numbers of e-mails daily, meet deadlines, and produce quarterly profits. These pressures are real and tend to reinforce a short-term, restless mindset, but reflective practices help people develop a counterbalancing mindset that is broader, calmer, and less reactive, so they become less likely to succumb to the old beliefs and behaviors that these normal pressures bolster.

The practices we offer you in the pages ahead are designed to shift individual and organizational beliefs and behaviors. Some of the individual practices can also be used organization-wide, and others can be used system-wide. Some are akin to the group exercises and personal mastery practices that underpin Peter Senge's *The Fifth Discipline* or Otto Scharmer's *Theory U*—practices that are designed to open up organizations to their existing belief structure and create an opening for new beliefs to take root.[44]

The practices we present are a small set of all those that exist. We chose them because we thought they would be most helpful for starting the process of linking spirituality to flourishing. While it helps to have an explicit and clear mandate for flourishing and for reflective processes from the top of the business, and while it's encouraging if at least some of the people undertaking and supporting reflective practices are in positions of power in the organization, this work basically rests on every individual, here and now. Many of us may believe that without top-level support for flourishing and for bringing reflective practices to the workplace, a firm will struggle longer and harder before it wakes up to the need to respond to voices and perspectives coming from below or from outside the organization. Nonetheless, we can't sit on our hands until such top-level support is assured. We must begin the work here and now, where we are.

In a 2000 *Fast Company* article on "tempered radicals,"[45] Debra Meyerson speaks about leaders at a variety of levels and in various firms who are committed to authenticity and passionate about change. One of our group of authors was featured in that article and spoke about his passion for the environment and the disadvantaged. Although that agenda was quite unlike the agenda of the major auto manufacturer for which he was an executive, he had over time acquired the credibility to put his ideas in place. He accomplished this, in the terms mentioned earlier, by doing a good job of doing the hard work of carrying water and chopping wood. He delivered on the promised profits and produced high-quality vehicles while never taking his eyes off his larger vision of flourishing.

So here we are, back to looking at the road signs on this map we are creating: Our goal is a 150-year vision in which humans and all other species can flourish on the earth forever. We reframe sustainability as flourishing, pointing to transformation at all levels: thriving individuals, prosperous organizations, healthy global systems, and ultimately a flourishing planet. Those outcomes emanate from people who are able to experience a sense of connection to others and to the world around them, such that their thinking and action support caring for others. The result is not only implicitly more desirable but also more effective in producing the intended outcomes: business success in today's complex multi-stakeholder environments.

What can business people do to enable organizations to care for individuals and teams in ways that are transformative and lead to flourishing? What principles and practices are needed? We now turn to the reflective practices that are capable of fostering the change of perspectives that lies at the heart of this transformation.

CHAPTER 4

Introduction to
the Reflective Practices

As we began to collect reflective practices that support the flourishing enterprise, we discovered a core set of guiding principles that build on the emerging beliefs defined in the previous chapters. These principles, and their attendant practices, place us on the reinforcing loop of flourishing individuals, flourishing enterprise, and flourishing world.

The Five Principles

The case for beginning with the principles that underpin our thought processes is often attributed to the sage Lao-Tze, who spoke these words more than two thousand years ago:

> Watch your thoughts; they become words.
>
> Watch your words; they become actions.
>
> Watch your actions; they become habits.
>
> Watch your habits; they become character.
>
> Watch your character; it becomes your destiny.

The following five principles shape the internal dialogue that guides our thinking, words, actions, habits, and character in support of flourishing. They serve as a solid link between the ideas associated with flourishing and the reflective practices and actions that support it.

1. We are fundamentally interconnected with each other and with all species. Underneath all systems theory and most spiritual traditions is an assumption that all beings are but nodes on an interconnected web. None of us exists as a completely separate

entity. Thus, in a number of ways, what I do to you, I do to myself, and do to all life—a notion that echoes the African ethic of *Ubuntu*—"I am what I am because of who we all are."

2. Our beliefs shape our actions in the world. What we choose to do is a manifestation of our thinking, which in turn is driven by our beliefs and mental models. Our "being" shapes our "doing"—a reminder of the shovel work needed to uncover our Level 1 and Level 2 beliefs.

3. We can choose to act from love and caring rather than from fear. Although we often act on the basis of unconscious motivations, when we consciously choose the stance we wish to take, we realize we always have a fundamental choice: to act from our fears of what we don't want to happen, or alternatively, from our love of what we most cherish and want to create.

4. What we focus on expands. When we place our attention on what we most wish for, it grows in our consciousness and drives us to create the conditions for what we want, which makes our desired results more likely. Alternatively, when we place our attention on what we don't want, our fears tend to grow both in our consciousness and as a driver of our actions, oftentimes resulting in us unintentionally creating more of what we don't want.

5. Flourishing depends on action coming from deep wisdom. Flourishing at all levels—individual, organizational, societal, and global—begins in actions that come from a connected, loving relationship with oneself, others, and all life. Such a way of being needs to be evident at all levels, regardless of one's role.

These principles can be seen in a variety of enterprise initiatives that connect, by design or not, to spirituality. The practices that the principles encourage have the potential to provide a natural shift of the enterprise toward flourishing. We share these principles in order

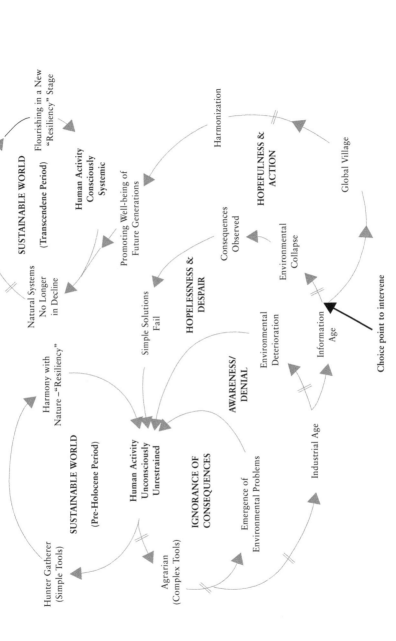

FIGURE 4.1 Evolutionary Track to Flourishing

SOURCE: Adapted from Roger Saillant and Jeremy Bendik-Keymer, "Sustainability, Trajectory and Possibility," *International Journal of Ethical Leadership, n (2012): 83.

to invite new partners into dialogue and to spark fresh ideas for reflective practices beyond those we recommend, practices that can create flourishing business in service of a flourishing world.

Our busy modern lives may make it difficult to hold to these principles, but at the very least it is good to lay them before us. In the light of ongoing and accelerating breakthroughs in technology, Roger Saillant and Jeremy Bendik-Keymer remind us:

Our stories about our technological power surged ahead while at the same time our spiritual connection to all things natural diminished. The natural world was a world to be subjugated and controlled, and those who wanted to reverse the damaging trends were not only met with resistance but began to feel hopeless and fell into despair which engendered a feeling of helplessness. . . . although we will never be able to restore lost natural systems to their original state existent in the Holocene period . . . there is the possibility that we can arrest the global decline in natural systems and establish an entirely new balance with the natural world."[1]

The systems diagram in Figure 4.1 captures this progressive movement of humanity's impacts on natural systems and the possibility of our collective response to re-establish a more balanced relationship with the world around us.

The technological advances that have improved our productivity and made our lives easier in uncountable ways have also had the unintended consequence of taking us away from the spiritual experiences that were more common in earlier, less technologically driven times. As we have enabled ourselves to go faster and with an ever-increasing amount of information available, our minds and hearts have gotten out of balance and our ability to flourish has become threatened. We are also coming to see that it is through the spiritual domain that we might reclaim some of that essential balance. It is a possibility based on the idea of maintaining an openness to life at all levels, rather than a project for encapsulating, dominating, and exploiting life.

What We Mean by Reflective Practices

The term *reflective practices* refers to practices that some might think of as spiritual, such as meditation, as well as those that might be characterized as secular, such as journaling and immersion in nature. Realizing that many "secular" or "nonspiritual" practices can lead us into spiritual territory (for instance, journaling as a regular practice can lead to a heightened sense of connectedness and to a more centered way of being), we want to capture the broadest set of practices that can lead to the spiritual experience of connectedness. This mix of both spiritual and nonspiritual practices capable of leading to spiritual experiences does not require us to align with any particular religious tradition—Eastern or Western. As an example, the practice of *Remembrance,* taken from a Sufi practice and detailed in Chapter 5, may strike the reader as a form of prayer associated with practices from other faith traditions whereas others would consider it a secular meditative practice.

It might help to say a little more about the term *practice*. We know what a *medical practice* or *legal practice* is: an endeavor in which certain professional standards and prescribed routines are applied consistently. Most of us have experience with practice from our childhood: practicing music or athletics or a craft or other creative endeavor. We may even have maintained that practice throughout our life. We know the answer to the playful question, "How do you get to Carnegie Hall?" The answer is, "Practice, practice, practice." That idea applies here. Reflective practices impact us, and the world around us, because of practice.

These regularly repeated reflective practices are powerful in opening our ways of thinking and being—in part because of their repetition. Scientists tell us that they change the folds of our brains,[2] providing evidence of their tangible neurophysiological impacts. Their power comes from the patterns of repetition that make the practice second nature. That's why people often say they have a "practice of meditation" or a "practice of time alone in nature." That's not to say that one can't in a moment do something that will shift thinking and open new possibilities, such as focus on breathing, or shift from statements to questions, or attune to body sensations.³ But it is sustained practice of a more complex nature that allows us to respond more consistently and more wisely to life's surprises.

Malcolm Gladwell, in his book *Outliers*,⁴ cites extraordinary performance and success across a wide range of fields, with examples including Bill Gates, the Beatles, and hockey stars. What is the condition for such success that he sees across all these fields? Ten thousand hours of practice. That's what is required for mastery: ten thousand hours. Others who have studied extraordinary success have landed on the same number.⁵ But lest one panic at the thought of adding ten thousand hours of activity to the work already before us: these are hours over a lifetime of doing what we already do, but doing it differently—in a more disciplined, focused way—for instance, practicing a more powerful way of thinking, a wiser way of responding to challenge, or a more constructive practice for dealing with conflict.

The reflective practices we set out in the next chapters are a sample of those we have found powerful in sustaining a sense of individual flourishing, in our own lives and in the lives of those around us. We have seen them increase the effectiveness of the teams and organizations with which we work, and in other enterprises we know about. All of these practices meet several of the following criteria:

1. Solid research and documentation support their power in helping individuals, teams, organizations, and systems flourish.

2. One or more of us were able to offer our own firsthand experience with their transformational power.

3. They add a spiritual component, as defined earlier, to sustainability—or better yet, to flourishing—efforts.

4. They offer the possibility of lasting transformation at one or more levels: individual, team, organizational, and system.

5. They instill a persistent, lasting orientation, or way of being, that nurtures flourishing at all those levels.

Although the practices and practical tools offered here can make an immediate difference in the quality of life and work in our organizations, we should be clear that we are relentlessly and patiently pointing toward a distant destination that is much larger. We are offering a very long view: a line of sight to a place and time where all living beings can flourish on the earth. The processes offered here can move us along that path one step at a time; yet each step, whether for an individual or a team, or for the next generation, is a step on a steep and compelling collective journey.

We invite you to build on the ideas from the preceding chapters as you sift through the practices to which we now turn. These practices—both practical and visionary—are part of a toolkit for constant renewal and purposeful growth that helps us stay the course toward flourishing.

CHAPTER 5

Foundational, Individual Practices

How do individual reflective tools and practices strengthen a sense of personal flourishing?

The reflective practices we describe in this chapter, some familiar to you, others not—mindfulness meditation, journaling, artwork—allow each of us to step back, absorb important insights, and see connections that would otherwise be invisible to us. They allow us to digest the realities of the world around us. Such practices ultimately allow us to engage more fully and more authentically in any endeavor. They can produce a sense of spiritual wellness that fuels passion, persistence, commitment, and ongoing connection.

You may find yourself curious about where these various practices come from. Some of them, such as journaling, have historical and cultural roots. Others, such as nature-immersion practices, are rooted in the science of biology, as well as in teachings of the indigenous peoples of the Americas. Some come from creative practitioners who have designed them, or from theorists who have shaped a new way of seeing things, and then designed practices for people to use to enter that new world. Still others grew out of contemporary research. A number are secular variants on spiritual practices.

Lest we be tempted to put the spiritual world on a strategic planning track or to make this process a forced march, we are reminded that the investment in practice is an ever-evolving process. Each of us makes choices to invest our energies in key practices that increase our capacity for flourishing and for contributing to the flourishing of others. We each choose to take a first step, then another, in order to move in a productive, effective direction. As one wise colleague reminds us, the soul (or if you prefer, the spiritual dimension) can spot being forced and manipulated from forty paces.[1] So our approach to introducing practices to others and into work environments needs to be inquiring and invitational—much like the eye doctor who gently says, as he tries first one lens then another: Does this help? How about this one?

The intentional change methodology of our colleague Richard Boyatzis provides a way of choosing among these lenses, of choosing among these practices and creating time for them, in the same way one carves out time to get physical exercise. Most busy executives, realizing that their physical health is a cornerstone of their leadership, make time for a disciplined physical work-out process. The same is needed for these reflective practices. We need the same commitment to finding time for them that we have for the gym.

In this book we provide detailed, disciplined processes in the spirit of inviting you to enter more powerfully into the game, knowing that what flows from the invitation can be a range of results—changes in ways of behaving, changes in ways of thinking, changes in our ease of relating to people, and an ever increasing commitment to flourishing at all levels.

Some would say that these practices offer us, first of all, the increased self-knowledge from which springs "right action" in the world.

They acknowledge this timeless wisdom: know thyself. And as Welsh poet David Whyte would remind us, it is wise to start with that first and often difficult step. His poem "Start Close In" reminds us to

Start close in,
   don't take the second step
   or the third,
   start with the first
   thing
   close in,
   the step you don't want to take.[2]

This process of disciplined expansion of our knowledge of ourselves is at the heart of personal mastery, one of the five disciplines of organizational learning identified by Peter Senge.[3] Personal mastery combines two dimensions that lead to individual and organizational flourishing: self-knowledge and an increasingly strong sense of calling or purpose or vision. Although people may hold different visions, we have settled on, and invite you into, the following expansive one: the 150-year vision of humans and all other species flourishing on the earth forever.

Along with strengthening our self-knowledge, the reflective practices in this chapter also help us see beyond ourselves to the connections among us and around us. From the growing awareness of those connections is likely to come a greater sense of caring for self, for others, for living things, and for the planet. And from that sense of caring is likely to emerge commitment, deeper meaning in life, and for many, a stronger sense of calling.

But notice the choice of words: "is likely to emerge." This path toward flourishing is a probabilistic one, not a deterministic one. In a deterministic dynamic, where we can ensure predictability, if we do one specific thing, we always get the same result—for instance, in manufacturing, if we get the inputs right, we always get a red Mustang convertible at the end of the assembly line. In the domain of human and spiritual dynamics, we are working with possibilities: we undertake these reflective practices, individually and collectively, with the understanding (supported by contemporary science) that they will increase the likelihood of the outcomes we seek. The practices increase the possibility of flourishing at every level. The states of connection, caring, commitment, and calling are, in systems terms, a reinforcing dynamic. They help us know what is right to do, a notion that early twentieth-century environmentalist Aldo Leopold captures in his guidance about how to think about things in a system: "A thing is right when it tends to preserve the integrity, stability, and beauty of the biotic community. It is wrong when it tends otherwise."[4] Reflective practices produce an organic learning process that opens the likelihood of action toward a more hopeful future. And such action renews us and then returns us to the reflective processes that have increased our personal flourishing.

People have asked us what practices they can build into their lives as a beginning point for flourishing. What practices form an "on-ramp" of sorts to a more effective path, both personally and for our enterprise? The following practices that create the on-ramp of individual practice are possible starting points for those exploring this domain. For those who already have a reflective practice, the ones presented here provide ideas for how to deepen a practice or perhaps to begin another related, reinforcing practice. For instance, if we are already meditators, how might walking meditation in a natural setting create richer insights and a stronger sense of purpose for us? Or if we find music to be a powerful force, how might learning to play an instrument (or beginning to play it again) serve our increasing awareness? These are the kinds of questions to ask while considering the reflective practices that follow.

Meditation

The practice of meditation in spiritual communities and in the broader society has a long history, particularly in the East. It has seen significant growth over the past decades in Western culture, and some business organizations now offer opportunities, time, and space for employees to step out of the flow of work and meditate.[5] For some communities of leadership practice, such as the Buddhism-based ALIA (Authentic Leadership in Action), mindfulness meditation is a cornerstone of leadership practice. Some businesses have made the same judgment of its importance in developing their people: note the recent visible effort of a Google employee to teach meditation in a business setting.[6] Other business leaders are outspoken about the important role their meditation practice plays in their leadership: Aetna CEO Mark Bertolini, who created Aetna's mindfulness and yoga programs in 2010 and is himself a meditator, says of his multifaceted daily practice of morning yoga, "That's my wellness programme. It's helped me be more centered, more present." It may sound foreign to some of us, but it is a familiar cornerstone to him.

The concept of mindfulness dates from early Buddhist thought in the fourth and third centuries BC, but it has since become a practice followed by a variety of spiritual traditions. Contemporary Western conceptualizations of mindfulness focus on a state of awareness that is relaxed, open, and "in the moment"—meaning anchored in the present. The practice of mindfulness can involve a period of quiet reflection, or it can simply be about cultivating an awareness of one's self, environment, and others throughout the day. Mindfulness meditation asks that we simply practice being present to our thoughts and feelings, sit with them (literally a "sitting practice"), and establish an increasingly calm equanimity and presence to what the world offers us. Being present, open, and aware makes one more effective in any activity and provides a number of benefits, including improved health, better relationships, better self-regulation, and increased enjoyment of life.

Steve Jobs told his biographer, "If you just sit and observe, you will see how restless your mind is. If you try to calm it, it only makes it worse, but over time, it does calm, and when it does, there's room to hear more subtle things—that's when your intuition starts to blossom and you start to see things more clearly and be in the present more. Your mind just slows down, and you see a tremendous expanse in the moment. You see so much more than you could see before. It's a discipline; you have to practice it."[7]

Mindfulness meditation is about learning to experience life fully as it unfolds—moment by moment. Practitioners such as Jon Kabat-Zinn[8] see meditation as an invitation to wake up and become more aware of the world around us. It allows us to experience the fullness of life and to transform our relationship with the problems, fears, and stresses that we encounter on a daily basis. The experience of fullness keeps the challenges from controlling us and eroding our quality of life and the capacity for creativity. Mindfulness is not about running away or manipulating mental states. It's about facing daily life with ever-increasing levels of equanimity.

Through the practice of mindfulness, we learn to develop greater calmness, clarity, and insight in facing and embracing all of life's experiences, even life's trials, and to turn them into occasions for learning, growing, and deepening our strength and wisdom. David Gelles, writing in the *Financial Times*, says that meditation "isn't some passing fad sweeping middle management, or a pilot programme dreamed up by human resources." He goes on to describe long-term commitments to mindfulness and meditation programs made by corporations such as Aetna, General Mills, Target, and Google and their CEOs.[9] There is no doubt that these corporations are finding mindfulness relevant to business results. These practices help people learn to breathe consciously, manage their emotional stress more effectively, and quiet their minds, so that they function more effectively, think more clearly, and are more creative and productive. The bottom line is better business results.

Whatever the form of meditation, however, its value is that it strengthens the individual's awareness of the thoughts and feelings that are moving through him or her. One can come to see those thoughts and feelings as the weather of the soul or, for those who do not believe the soul exists, as the weather of the emotions. It is this awareness and the attendant ability to choose alternative patterns of thought and feeling that over time create a genuine steadiness and centeredness in the face of life's and the organization's challenges.

The ability to work reflectively with the mind and emotions is a foundational practice in linking spirituality and flourishing. It also has the power to keep us from being reactive in ways that ratchet up troubles and produce even greater problems. In the words of Thich Nhat Hanh, the leader of a movement called Engaged Buddhism, "Don't just do something; sit there," which points us to the value of sitting meditation.

Although the idea appears silly at first, given our crazily busy circumstances, sometimes "just sitting there" is exactly what is needed if we are to discern the most effective action and not take a mindless step that in systems terms comes back to haunt us.

Mindful Action and Flow

The concept of flow, pioneered by Mihaly Csikszentmihalyi,[10] describes those situations in which individuals experience both heightened enjoyment and improved performance through absorption or engrossment in a particular activity. David Baker at Boeing talks about how flow plays into the company's thinking about the right assignments for people. They place people in alignment with their natural goals, interests, and skill levels. "Finding the right alignments creates magic. It engages people in their work. . . . When this happens the person is capable of reaching states of 'flow' with outstanding performance. Our people have reported to us that instead of being exhausted, the work takes on energizing qualities."

Flow can be considered a state of optimal performance and can bring a sense of exhilaration and deep enjoyment as a person's mind and body are stretched to their limits in an effort to accomplish something that is difficult and worthwhile. Hence, both mindful action and flow each serve to improve performance and overall joy.

Flow often occurs in situations where people are operating at levels that for them are above average in challenge and to which they must bring above-average skills. It is quite common to experience flow when playing a sport or a musical instrument at a high level of mastery. Athletes and musicians refer to this experience with phrases such as "being in the zone" or "deep play." In its most central formulation, the state of flow involves intense concentration on the present, the merging of action and awareness, the loss of self-consciousness, increased self-efficacy, temporal distortion, and enjoyment. Though we may think of flow being limited to star athletes who are "in the zone," each of us can experience flow during work activities, creative projects, or hobbies. We step into them and they begin to feel like play. We gain intrinsic value just through performing them. So an important individual practice for many people may be an athletic, creative, or artistic endeavor that opens them to flow.

Remembrance and Transformational Problem Solving

Many other personal practices can help us move through challenging dynamics in a productive and healthy way. One such practice is *remembrance*. It is particularly effective in bringing out the best in people who are facing complex or personally daunting challenges.

Relatively unknown in Western society and taken from an ancient Sufi tradition, remembrance can provide a transformational experience with lasting impact, enabling us to see ourselves and a given situation in a different light. It involves repeating the name of God or another phrase or word that is in some way sacred to the person speaking it and that connects to the person's deepest source of creativity, inspiration, and wisdom.[11] The repetition allows one to let go of chronic stress and reawakens a sense of inspiration, creativity, and possibility. It both strengthens us and provides guidance for whatever challenges and circumstances we face. It has universal application for those who desire a direct, intimate, and powerful connection to their personal understanding of the "source of all that is."

Remembrance assumes that life is a journey for which all of the most meaningful experiences we seek and all of the answers we need are treasures buried in our own hearts, waiting for us to remember them. The practice of repeating the sacred word heightens the person's innate positive qualities so that those qualities become more prevalent and natural ways of being, during both times of ease and times of difficulty. With practice, a person's positive qualities overcome or replace counterproductive qualities such as self-doubt, self-importance, arrogance, judgment, anxiety, and hopelessness, leaving them with an experience of deep wisdom, peace, compassion, patience, and internal strength—all qualities of a flourishing human being. Although the practice of remembrance can at first sound too easy or almost "magical," serious business people who have invested themselves fully in it have found it leads to remarkable results.

The practice of remembrance made a real difference for one executive when he was looking for a way to get over his distracting and persistent upset over a failed business partnership. His experiment of investing 30 minutes daily, for thirty days, in the practice of remembrance bore startling results. The one most surprising to him was that he began to smile naturally, for what seemed to him no apparent reason. It was the signal that he had moved beyond the setback.

He relayed his experience to a corporate CEO who was at the end of her rope about a series of employee accountability issues. She had also admitted in passing that she had been having severe long-lasting headaches twice a week for twenty years. To his suggestion that she try remembrance the CEO said, "I'll try anything." She chose the word *Elohim* as her sacred word and the two sat together in silence for fifteen minutes in remembrance. When she opened her eyes, she said that what she'd noticed was that somehow the sound of the rain on the window had made her aware of something much more unusual—what felt to her like a light coming into her heart and melting a mountain of sadness. She laughed at the image of the sun in Oregon during the winter. Later she would say that her openness to trying anything and being at the end of her rope had been exactly what she needed in order to receive the benefits of this reflective experience. During the following months of continued practice of remembrance on her own every day, she one day realized she had become completely free of the pain of the ever-recurrent headaches.

Practices such as remembrance increase our capacity to listen to ourselves, to the subtle wisdom within that we often overlook in our rush and our busyness, as well as to others, to the subtle cues they give us about what matters to them and about what they are seeing. We are better able to be present to circumstances, whether joyous or challenging, without retreating, fleeing, or overreacting.

The power of reflection (particularly for leaders) is at the heart of Richard Boyatzis and Annie McKee's work in *Resonant Leadership*.[12] They trace the ways that reflective practices, and stepping out of the busyness, even for a moment, can be a critical move in a business situation. The momentary reflective "time-out" can, by increasing our awareness of self, allow us to be more attuned to others and more aware of workplace dynamics, and therefore result in a leadership process and an organization that are steadier and more effective. The authors suggest that the only way off the gerbil wheel of frantic busyness, the sacrifice cycle with its destructive impact on the health of individual and organization—or as we would say, on the flourishing of individuals and the organization—is to take that difficult first step into such reflective space. Showing the courage to do just that not only increases personal health but also can help lead to team and organizational flourishing.

What is our warning signal that we are stuck in a nonproductive rut? How do we make the shift to a smarter path? One answer builds on what we have observed about the practice of remembrance and has been incorporated into a process called Transformational Problem Solving (TPS).

TPS is based on two assumptions found in the practice of remembrance: (1) human beings are innately good, and (2) unwelcome developments in life can either throw us into a state of forgetting our innate goodness or, if we take an alternative path, those developments can deepen our experience of our goodness and make us more effective. The result depends on the path we take. With practice, the alternative path of TPS leads one to experience a more natural, empowered, and resilient way of being, thereby changing our default response from one that entangles us to one that frees us. In doing so, it shifts our narrative about what's possible each time a difficult situation arises.

The process begins with our realizing that the mind often resists dealing with the unappealing moments of life. It could accept them and the emotions we have about them, but it doesn't want to.

Acceptance does not mean welcoming the undesirable moment. It simply means being present to it long enough to access our highest intentions and the wisdom we need to work through this challenging situation and the obstacles associated with it. Resisting the situation takes us out of our present moment and results in a dreaded "here we go again" view of the future. The "here we go again" thinking then becomes a self-fulfilling belief, with two thoughts: (1) our intentions cannot be realized and (2) compromising ourselves is inevitable. When our mind spins in limited thinking and worry, we have, in the language of this practice, "lost heart," at least momentarily. If we do not recover quickly, we end up struggling with our experience of reality and taking compromised actions that create more of what we do not want—a reinforcing loop of negativity.

The practice of remembrance that is embedded in TPS assists us in accessing the wisdom in our hearts so we can find our highest intentions and move through our challenging situation with inspired action. Figure 5.1 provides a visual overview of the step-by-step approach to transforming our way of being each time we have a problem so that we can resolve it from our highest level of consciousness.

As we become proficient in this approach to problem solving, our capacities become stronger and we become more resilient, until we are able to maintain our composure more often and in more difficult dynamics. We discover that we do not need to struggle with our unwelcome moments in life, and that the wisdom evident in remembrance and TPS is always available to us. We are able to step beyond what we see as problems by accepting what occurs, reflecting on the path we are choosing, and reducing the time and energy we lose in an experience of struggle.

A case in point: A leader who faced grilling by members of a powerful business panel practiced remembrance and TPS until she was viscerally calmer. Remembrance helped her to side-step her historical fears of public speaking and to operate from the awareness that she was serving a critical purpose. She could bring to mind her

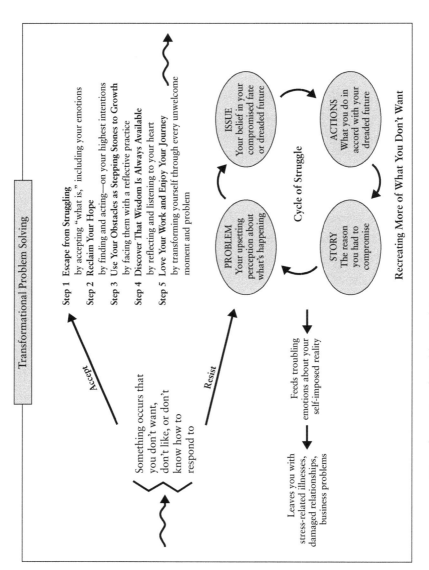

Transformational Problem Solving

Step 1 Escape from Struggling
by accepting "what is," including your emotions

Step 2 Reclaim Your Hope
by finding and acting—on your highest intentions

Step 3 Use Your Obstacles as Stepping Stones to Growth
by facing them with a reflective practice

Step 4 Discover That Wisdom Is Always Available
by reflecting and listening to your heart

Step 5 Love Your Work and Enjoy Your Journey
by transforming yourself through every unwelcome moment and problem

Accept

Resist

Something occurs that you don't want, don't like, or don't know how to respond to

Leaves you with stress-related illnesses, damaged relationships, business problems

Feeds troubling emotions about your self-imposed reality

ISSUE
Your belief in your compromised fate or dreaded future

ACTIONS
What you do in accord with your dreaded future

PROBLEM
Your upsetting perception about what's happening

STORY
The reason you had to compromise

Cycle of Struggle

Recreating More of What You Don't Want

FIGURE 5.1 Transformational Problem Solving

SOURCE: Copyright © LionHeart Consulting Inc, 2005. Used with permission.

well-known accomplishments and her experience that provided her with what she needed to answer the panel's questions effectively. Once she turned to remembrance, she navigated through the challenge, providing clear testimony, which allowed for success and evident appreciation. Her added confidence enabled her to approach other business leaders successfully that same afternoon. She experienced a reinforcing flourishing loop driven by reflective practice.

Such examples of overcoming problems using remembrance and TPS often sound relatively routine to others, and even to ourselves, once we have effectively worked through the problem and stepped beyond our disempowering beliefs. However, the value of this process lies in the hard truth that every one of us occasionally gets wound up inside with a problem that has us lose heart. And each time we effectively move through such a problem by using a transformational process, we reinforce our experience of our innate creative abilities. We strengthen our trust that we have access to the wisdom and strength we need to face our toughest challenges in a way that is consistent with our highest intentions. Instead of hesitating or losing heart when problems and obstacles to our dreams inevitably arise, we stop and notice our momentary discomfort, then shift our awareness before taking action. This practice uses each problem or moment of discomfort or distress as a place to take a momentary time-out in order to deepen our reliance on reflective experiences that nurture our sense of confidence and allow us to become a more flourishing human being.

Journaling

Journal writing is another way to increase our awareness of the thought processes that may be tangling us up. There is something about the disciplined process of taking note of our life and our insights that increases our capacity to take seriously our own feeling and thinking processes. It helps us to see and admit our blindspots. We can see more clearly, and over time we become more willing to speak the truth about our perspective. Writing regularly in a journal strengthens our sense of personal authorship and voice.

It is no accident that over the centuries journaling has been a practice of travelers, scientists, leaders, public figures, poets, and explorers. Reading others' journals has been an important source of cultural learning for us as a species. Many know of the journals of the explorer Sir Ernest Shackleton and his twenty-eight scientists and sailors who returned, all safe, all well, with journals (and photos and movies) in hand after being stranded in Antarctica for 497 days from 1914 to 1916. It is their journals that give us the details of their experience, but more important to their survival was that the journals allowed them to give in-the-moment meaning to their experience and instill within and among themselves an unrelenting expectation that they would return alive. The journals carried their vision, their hope.

Contemporary research has shown that writing in a journal about making our way through a difficult experience promotes individual flourishing. Research shows that it has a lasting positive impact on the immune system.[13] But for our purposes, the power of journaling lies in its ability to help us take note of our experiences, learn from them, speak honestly of them, and be increasingly aware of the subtle information and connections that surround us all.

Journaling can take many forms. Julia Cameron advocates the practice of "morning pages" in which one writes several pages without editing, and without judgment, about whatever is on one's mind.[14] It can be a form of automatic writing. For others, including one member of our group, the journaling process is a structured practice—in this case, decades long. Having begun with the guidance of Ira Progoff's structured journal,[15] she starts each day with a half-hour of writing, noting what is carried forward from the day before (a form of what in the military is often called an "after action review"), being present to the moment of writing (What does she see, feel, hear, in this moment?) and noting the intentions she holds for the day (What is she committed to, in this day, no matter what?). This simple, disciplined daily journaling process has instilled in her a pattern of greater awareness of the world, and a sensitivity to her own patterns of behavior and thinking. It has also been the opening to much of her creative work—including her practice as a poet. She laughingly notes that through the journaling process alone (not including other practices such as handling difficult work conversations, negotiations, dialogue, music, walks in nature, and kayaking) she has put in more than half of her ten thousand hours of reflective practice.

Although many of us are already inveterate note-takers, it is worth mentioning that a journal turns us from taking notes on the world to taking notes on our own interior reality: our thoughts, our emotions, our framing of things, the meaning we make of what is going on around us, the stories we tell ourselves. It is a mirror of the inner life that we may not otherwise even acknowledge that we have.

Perhaps the most critical capacity strengthened by journaling is the ability to notice, particularly to pay attention to subtleties that one might otherwise miss. The journal strengthens awareness of one's self, of others, and of the natural world. It taps into the still, quiet spiritual dimension of the individual. Journal activities can be individual, and they can also be built into teamwork, and even into systems processes, to increase their impact—as in the case of a systems process that we describe later in which participants quickly, without overthinking, respond to a series of provocative questions about their own creativity.

Journal work can also connect a person to flourishing in the natural world by focusing the journal work on something in nature. One of the authors regularly invites executives to take their journal and go out into nature. Encouraged to wander around outside, in a variant of the learning process of the Native American Oneida Nation, each individual finds some natural object that catches their attention, for whatever reason—perhaps a particular tree or an unusual rock. They have been instructed to sit with that natural object for half an hour, writing in their journal the details of what they observe about it, particularly what it might have to teach them about any change or challenges they face. After the half-hour of quiet writing, the executives return to the room and gather in twos or threes to share their insights about their natural object.

This ability of nature to provide clues to help us solve the problems we are facing is the stock-in-trade of a powerful community of scientists—the Biomimicry Guild—and is described in the writing of Janine Benyus.[16] Numerous organizations, including Nike and Interface Inc., both famous for their sustainability initiatives, have engaged teams of biologists in this process of learning from nature to make breakthroughs in design.

As far out as the process of sitting with a natural object seems initially, most executives appreciate the half-hour of quiet, and the chance to draw links between nature and their own experiences. In one yearlong leadership program for construction firm executives that met for a week each quarter, after the initial week's half-hour journal exercise with the natural object, the executives asked to be able to sit with their natural object again each week that they met. One executive, who was struggling with a very difficult dynamic at work, took the facilitator aside after the second period of journaling about a dried-out creek bed and said quietly, "Someday the rains will come and wash all the crap out. But not today." That seemed to be the turning point for him in making a decision to stay with the company rather than leave it. He credited nature, and his journal, as his coach in making a good decision.

Nature Immersion

First, here is a thought about our increasingly precarious circumstances in the twenty-first century:

Cultures that do not recognize that human life and the natural world have a sacred dimension, an intrinsic value beyond a monetary value, cannibalize themselves until they die. They ruthlessly exploit the natural world and the members of their society in the name of progress or collapse, blind to the fury of their own self-destruction.[17]

There are practices of simply being in nature that in and of themselves can create a level of connection with the natural world and a sense of its sacred dimension. Over time, from those experiences grows a commitment, a deeper caring, or what some would term a calling to be in service of that natural world. A number of scientific studies have shown the remarkable, and measurable, extent of this connection, under the heading of Attention Restoration Theory.[18]

The simple first step is to get out of the house or office and find ourselves in a natural setting. Or perhaps go running with a dog! One of us who has had a strong affinity to being outside in nature rescued a "red and white" Siberian named Kira. His several-times-a-week practice is to run along the trail with Kira as she goes hunting. She inhales the air, stops to sniff the brush, and attempts to sprint after birds and ground squirrels. At the other end of the springy leash, he attempts to follow Kira's lead, sprinting and slamming to a stop as she does. He hopes to be as present and open to the moment as possible, immersed in and paying close attention to the natural beauty, Kira's instinctive behavior, and the abundant wildlife.

Experiences in nature can indeed foster a sense that it is there that we are at home. The contemporary leadership-and-change model known as "presencing" was fostered by an experience of letting go of assumptions and ideas and being immersed in a natural setting. Multi-day Outward Bound experiences have usually included a "solo" in nature, a time when one is alone in a natural setting for an extended period. It is a way of understanding our capacity to be at home in the natural world that is much more lasting than just talking about it.

Of course we are not alone in these discoveries. A teacher from the Native American Oneida Nation invites corporate leaders to explore change by going out in nature. In a related practice, a leader from another North American native tribe has executives find one square foot of meadow and sit with it, in order to become increasingly aware of the richness, complexity, and detail, the subtleties of that one small piece of earth. There is a poetic notion that to know something and love it we must sit with it for a time in silence. This knowing involves a deeper kind of listening that is perhaps true not only for a square foot of earth, but also for knowing and caring about each other.

Art and Aesthetics

Art and aesthetics provide a broad domain of experience that engages our right brain and our deeper wisdom, thus helping us to move beyond the highly analytic modes of being and acting that are so prevalent and sometimes limiting in our work in business. Here we start by zooming in on one particular example, Zen drawing, before considering other forms of art-based reflective practices.

Zen drawing reminds us how often our fixed preconceptions of what something looks like or of what is going on in a given situation keep us from seeing what is really in front of us. Taken from the work of Frederick Franck,[19] this simple art exercise gives us a chance to overturn our preconceived ideas about what we are seeing and at the same time to break through our judgments about our own "art skills."

The process is to put pencil to paper and draw something without looking at the pencil or the paper, while keeping our eyes glued to the object we are drawing and never wavering from it. This unwavering focus is the beginning of learning to see what is actually in front of us. It gives us a chance to step away from our overloaded switchboard, fed by noise, agitation, and visual stimuli. It establishes an island of silence, an oasis of undivided attention.

When you have finished sketching, take a look at your work. You may be tempted to judge what you have drawn, but observe how this practice allows you to "get" the essence of the object, whether a tree or a rock or a branch, in a way that your neat, romantic no-tions of the object does not. As you look at your drawing, what do you find surprising about it? What is different from your preconceptions? What does the tree, and your picture of it, have to teach you?

For those who panic at the very idea of having to draw, there is a way to work with the power of images without having to draw a thing. The Visual Explorer, a tool of the Center for Creative Leadership,[20] shifts us from words to images and in doing so provides access to new insights. The process is simple: After clarifying a dream or goal that each person holds for the future, participants walk among a large number of 8 ½ by 11-inch visual images spread out on the floor and choose one that "speaks to them," that catches their attention. It need not relate directly to their dream for the future. They then return to their dream idea with the picture in hand and write about the image that has caught their attention. What attracted them to it? And what might it suggest about their dream for the future? Next they take turns introducing the image and their reflections on it to two partners. Finally, they invite their partners' further reflections on what the image might suggest about the dream.

Poetry and Evocative Language

It's not unusual for organizational leaders to start a meeting or an all-hands gathering with an inspiring quote or poem. They under-stand instinctively the power of a line from a poem to help people be present and focused. Perhaps the most famous example of the power of a poem to sustain a person is the experience of Nelson Mandela, for whom the poem "Invictus" allowed him to keep going when all he wanted to do was lie down. The poem was Mandela's lifeline in prison and thereafter. It ends with these words:" I am the master of my fate: I am the captain of my soul."[21]

The work of business isn't all that far from the world of poetry: some quite famous contemporary poets were also business executives. John Coleman, on the Harvard Business Review's Blog Network,[22] notes that when Wallace Stevens, a Pulitzer Prize winner and one of America's greatest poets, was offered a prestigious faculty position at Harvard, he turned it down saying he didn't want to give up his position as vice president of the Hartford Accident and Indemnity Company. He is not alone: Dana Gioia, a Stanford Business School graduate and former General Foods executive, notes in *Can Poetry Matter?* that English poet T. S. Eliot spent a decade at Lloyds Bank of London. Poetry may seem a bit off the main path of business. But if we miss out on poetry, Coleman says, "We overlook a genre that could be valuable to our personal and professional development." Sidney Harman, founder of Harman International Industries, once told the *New York Times,* "I used to tell my senior staff to get me poets as managers. Poets are our original systems thinkers. They look at our most complex environments and they reduce the complexity to something they begin to understand." Coleman continues:

Business leaders live in multifaceted, dynamic environments. Their challenge is to take that chaos and make it meaningful and understandable. Reading and writing poetry can exercise that capacity, improving one's ability to better conceptualize the world and communicate it—through presentations and through writing—to others. . . . Poetry can teach us to infuse life with beauty and meaning. A challenge in modern management can be to keep ourselves and our colleagues invested with wonder and purpose."

One of this book's authors, a poet who works as a leadership consultant, has been repeatedly surprised by the executives who take her aside and say, "I write poetry too, but don't tell anybody."

Sustainability as flourishing demands systems thinking, and clear thinking, as well as a feel for wonder and purpose. Working with poetry, individually and in teams, can increase that creativity and systems thinking. But how to do it?

It's easy for colleagues to work together with a poem in a way that is natural and fosters insight and a strong sense of connection: Choose a powerful and simple poem that you care about. It might be about commitment or sustainability or any other topic that poses an important question to each of you. One poem famous for doing that is Robert Frost's "The Road Not Taken." Provide everyone with a copy and have someone volunteer to read it aloud. Have a second reading by another volunteer. Then invite everyone to journal in silence about what stands out for them in the poem, what catches their eye—a word, a phrase, an image, an idea. Next, in groups of four, one at a time and without interruption, have people reflect out loud about what touches them in the poem and what it asks of them. Then have everyone return to the full group and discuss what in the poem seems most powerful to them and how it relates to the challenges they face—for instance, the challenges of flourishing.

Searching for poems to work with in organizations? Three good sources are *Teaching with Fire, Leading from Within,* and *Good Poems.*[23]

Music

What about music? How might we use it? One example is actually singing. Don't panic (although almost everyone does, at first, which is why it's powerful). Why would we want to sing?

Singing connects us to our voice. The practice of speaking from our natural voice requires knowing that voice, recognizing it, treasuring it. It is useful to practice with it, as if with an instrument, so we have the courage to be present publically with our very real, authentic voice. Maybe it is safest to sing in the shower, but that is just a starting place.

Voice coach Claude Stein leads groups of corporate executives through an exercise in which they sing a song about a place that means a great deal to them. Small groups of four executives sit knee to knee in a room, each one creating a song about a place and singing it, haltingly, sometimes Johnny one-note style, but nonetheless singing it, to three colleagues. It is an exercise in risk-taking, authenticity, and courage—being willing to be in one's own authentic voice, singing about something that really matters to us.

When people confront their fear of singing in public (as when we confront any limiting fear) and actually do sing about something that matters to them, they break through the inhibitions that keep them from being in their voice and speaking authentically of what matters to them in a business sense. They are suddenly able to speak openly and naturally about their commitments. In their work presentations, their voice is freed.

Choosing an Individual Practice

For those who have long had some kind of reflective practice (meditation or any other), the next step may be to bring that practice to the work of flourishing, to the intersection of the 150-year cathedral-building project of contributing to a world in which humans and all life can flourish on the earth forever. It may be journaling about deep connections. It may be a walking meditation in nature. Whatever, it is, it is about discovering novel ways to link one's existing practice to flourishing.

For others who have been toiling in the vineyard of "creating a better world," who find themselves too busy in the service of a compelling cause to take time out, and for whom a reflective practice is new territory, the research of Richard Boyatzis, mentioned earlier, offers a map for identifying a reflective practice and a strategy for finding the space and time for it. We point you toward Boyatzis' work because busy individuals can use it to create a path that can further open the spiritual domain, which is the domain we believe is so essential to making progress toward flourishing. Boyatzis' approach can help busy people integrate reflective practice into a busy schedule,[24] thereby enhancing their emotional, spiritual, and appreciative intelligences and helping them behave in ways that foster positivity, resonant relationships, and flourishing. It can help them on behalf of the compelling causes that have kept them so busy, and stressed, and unreflective.

A Note on Leadership Development

As we turn from foundational practices that strengthen flourishing in individuals to practices that strengthen flourishing in teams and organizations, we find a critical bridge linking the two: the many leaders who create the conditions for flourishing teams and organizations. This is a bridge that leaders at all levels bring into being through their actions. It is a bit like the poet Antonio Machado's notion: "Traveler there is no road. We build the road by walking."[25]

For leaders to provide that quality of leadership—leadership that allows, supports, and practices reflection, and that holds a systems perspective—some leaders put themselves into intentionally mind-stretching situations. That's the story of Walmart CEO Lee Scott's experience of immersing himself in an ecological system (described in the next section) and inviting experiences outside of his usual leadership role. Such experiences can strengthen key competencies required to lead the flourishing enterprise: emotional intelligence, spiritual intelligence, and appreciative intelligence—three ideas that we underscore as we turn toward practices for organizational flourishing.

System Immersion

Lee Scott's experience in what one of our group has called *system immersion* occurred in a carefully designed and facilitated CEO field trip. Often this process is associated with the term *study groups,* which is familiar to European executives. Such an experience provides them with a natural and inescapable sense of connection to the larger system and to the goal of flourishing. It supplies a setting for learning—for observation, dialogue, and deep reflection and enables executives and decision-makers to

- Experience, connect to, gain deep understanding of, and appreciate relevant sustainability topics
- Meet and engage in dialogue with stakeholders on the front lines of key issues
- Be in an environment and context that fosters inner reflection

The first immersion trip for Lee Scott was spent at the top of Mount Washington in a bunkhouse with climate scientists and other experts. Scott and the experts engaged in deep dialogue to understand what the experts were learning and to explore the implications of their findings for nature and society. To better understand the system from the perspective of other players, Scott also met with some third-generation maple syrup farmers who shared how climate change was affecting their trees and their business. The stories from the farmers describing the long-term change they were seeing and its impact were compelling. The trip occurred a few months prior to Walmart's announcement of its aggressive sustainability goals and strategies. One can only wonder at the link. Later trips organized for Walmart included experiences inside the Arctic Circle and with mountaintop coal mining in West Virginia.

The key to making system immersion a framework-shifting leadership development process is to make time for observation, reflection, deep dialogue, and other practices that help people to truly experience the whole system in multiple ways. System immersion is a powerful, life-changing way to learn, and not just for executives. It can be equally powerful for the young—shifting their thinking about the role they intend to play in the world. For those of us who hope our young business leaders will be prepared to join us and continue to carry us toward the goal of flourishing, system immersion is a promising foray into reflective practice.

Here's a case of such younger leaders at work: Participating in an action research approach from *Theory U,* a group of students chose for an environmental and social assessment a controversial planned construction project in South America: a hydroelectric plant already confronted by questions about its environmental impact. After interviews with a range of stakeholders, the students submitted their recommendations. The recommendations were turned down.

The students, however, were not deterred. Following the commitment that is at the heart of such reflective processes, they stayed deeply connected to their convictions. One of them wrote, "The impression I have is that we tend to rationalize our life as a way to protect and isolate ourselves. It is easier to think this is not our responsibility, someone else is responsible, and a good soul who will have what it takes to fix it. Except that, who are the good souls? At these moments, I dare to dream big, but I make sure that every one of us is present, committed, and daring to achieve the dream."

The students' tenacious sense of commitment, seen in this system immersion experience, was created because the process gave them space in which to dive deeply into their own reasons for living. Learning at a young age how to make decisions inspired by expanded awareness, they were able, in a systems sense, to see the "mighty oak in the acorn." It is possible to develop such leaders if one considers that the way people learn may influence their paths toward flourishing. And learning through immersion, with reflective processes built in, does just that.

Emotional Resonance, Resonant Leadership, and the Three Kinds of Critical Intelligence

Working effectively with processes of the sort we are describing here requires a set of resonant leadership skills or orientations—and multiple "intelligences": emotional intelligence, spiritual intelligence, and appreciative intelligence—that are not luxuries in organizations pursuing flourishing and effectiveness.

The work on resonance alerts us to why these intelligences matter. Daniel Goleman and Richard Boyatzis remind us that "leading effectively is, in other words, less about mastering situations—or even mastering social skill sets—than about developing a genuine interest in and talent for fostering positive feelings in the people whose cooperation and support you need."[26] They offer us a pragmatic process to help people learn how to connect to their positive emotions and use them for both self-development and the development of others. They call this capacity *emotional resonance*, and it can play a key role in fostering positivity and its accompanying effectiveness and happiness for teams, organizations, and systems. Emotional resonance

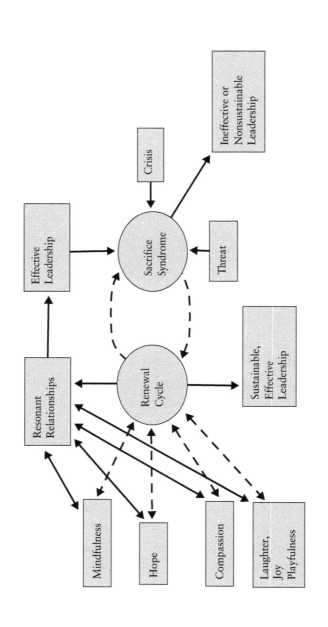

FIGURE 5.2 A Leadership Renewal Cycle Using Reflective Practices

SOURCE: Richard Boyatzis and Annie McKee, *Resonant Leadership: Renewing Yourself and Connecting with Others Through Mindfulness, Hope, and Compassion*. (Watertown MA: Harvard Business School Publishing, 2005).

Effects internal to (within) the leader are marked by dashed lines and arrows.

Social, interactive effects between the leader and others are marked by straight lines and arrows.

is especially important for leaders and others who set the emotional tone within a team, organization, or system. In this sense, emotional resonance and its manifestation in leaders is squarely aimed at enabling flourishing at every scale.[27]

In *Primal Leadership*,[28] Goleman, Boyatzis, and McKee lay out the neurophysiological link between the power of resonance and the success or failure of teams, organizations, and systems. Emotions are contagious and when they resonate—when they send out waves of energy and enthusiasm—they help teams, organizations, and systems to thrive. When negativity and dissonance dominate, effectiveness flounders. "Effective teams and powerful, positive organizational cultures do not happen by accident."[29] They are created by resonant leaders who employ emotional intelligence to motivate and nurture their employees. They do this by connecting with others using emotional intelligence competencies such as empathy (that is, sensing others' feelings and perspectives, and taking an active interest in others' concerns) and self-awareness.

In *Resonant Leadership*,[30] Boyatzis and McKee point out that in today's fast-paced, high-pressure business environment, many skillful leaders who are generally in resonance burn out and fall into dissonance. On the basis of this understanding of the leader's fall from resonance into dissonance, the authors provide a practical and field-tested framework for overcoming the vicious cycle of stress, sacrifice, and dissonance that afflicts many leaders. Their framework, shown in Figure 5.2, provides an alternative to the all-too-common constant sacrifice to workplace demands, suggesting how leaders can manage the sacrifice cycle to combat stress, avoid burnout, and renew themselves physically, mentally, and emotionally by using reflective practices that foster mindfulness, hope, and compassion.

EMOTIONAL INTELLIGENCE

Much has been written on emotional intelligence, a notion initially popularized by Goleman. In *Primal Leadership*, the framework that

Goleman, Boyatzis, and McKee offer includes four key dimensions: two personal dimensions—self-awareness and self-management—and two social dimensions—social awareness and relationship management. Reflective practice can be instrumental in improving emotional intelligence and, as we noted earlier, Google is using meditation for precisely this purpose.

SPIRITUAL INTELLIGENCE

Cindy Wigglesworth has developed a spiritual intelligence framework and skills-based assessment called the SQ 21 to help people assess forms of awareness that can be termed *spiritual*. In *SQ 21,* spiritual intelligence is defined as "the ability to behave with wisdom and compassion while maintaining inner and outer peace [equanimity] regardless of the circumstances." We were interested in understanding how this framework is influenced by and integrates with emotional intelligence. Our work with reflective practices leads us to propose that efforts to enhance emotional and spiritual intelligences are mutually reinforcing.

These two frameworks provide competency-based language and a novice-to-expert scaffolding that helps people assess their current status and define where they would like to be in their development, and then to plot reflective practices that might help them move in that direction. We turn now to a third and final framework, a kind of intelligence that underlies many of the practices we have sketched.

APPRECIATIVE INTELLIGENCE

Appreciative intelligence—which is not the same as Appreciative Inquiry, discussed in Chapter 3, yet shares many habits of thinking with it—complements the framework of emotional and spiritual intelligence and provides unique value for organizations. Developed by Tojo Thatchenkery and Carol Metzker, who define it as the ability to perceive the positive inherent generative potential within the present, appreciative intelligence is, in other words, the ability to see the mighty oak in the acorn.[31] They identify three components of appreciative intelligence: reframing, appreciating the positive, and seeing the future as it unfolds from the present. Appreciative intelligence leads to four qualities: persistence, conviction that one's actions matter, tolerance for uncertainty, and irrepressible resilience. Organizations that embrace appreciative intelligence have been shown, according to this research, to exhibit higher levels of innovation, more productive employees, greater ability to adapt to change, and ultimately, greater profit.

Thatchenkery and Metzker outline a process and some practices that people can use to enhance their appreciative intelligence. Similar to Richard Boyatzis' intentional change process, mentioned earlier, Thatchenkery and Metzker's process makes it possible to assess one's current level of appreciative intelligence and engage in regular practice to raise that level. The practices suggested include changing the stories we hold about our own realities, changing our reflections, changing our questions, and seeing diverse ideas.

By linking emotional resonance to these three types of intelligence—emotional, spiritual, and appreciative—and splicing in reflective practices that activate spiritual intelligence, business leaders have available to them a powerful arsenal of tools and methods with which to create a flourishing enterprise.

CHAPTER 6

Team and Organizational Practices

Having sketched individual reflective practices, and having noted the importance of leadership development that accepts and supports those practices, let us now turn to ways to root those practices in the work of teams and groups inside an organization. Anchoring them in the work of the organization opens a more "spiritual space" and a culture more welcoming of the spiritual dimension within the enterprise. A first step is to increase people's comfort with being who they are, with authenticity, and with sharing important truths about their lives.

Story Café

Inviting people into the practice of telling stories about a central theme or core value creates a much greater sense of connection among them, a valuing of one another's experiences, and an emotional reconnection with an important experience. It contributes to highlighting examples of values at work.

The process: Invite people into a Story Café—or just call it "conversational foursomes"—café-sized tables of four with round-robin storytelling focused on, for example, the theme of a time when nature touched them, or a time when they were able to speak courageously, or a place that has great meaning to them, or a time when they faced something unwelcome and years later were proud of how they handled it. The key is to choose a topic of value that everyone has likely experienced in one way or another. In a café on sustainability and flourishing, the topic of choice might be something like, "Think of a time when a connection to community or nature really touched you. Tell the story of what happened that touched you so."

Whatever the question, the format is always the same: First, have a few moments of silence as people take notes about their own story on the topic. Then, one at a time, with fifteen minutes for each person, have people tell their stories as their three colleagues just listen, wholeheartedly, without comment, soaking it up. Listening intently to stories carries with it the subtle and important message that we are the sole authority on what we have to say, on the story we are telling and on the meaning we give to it. Telling our story reminds us that we are the sole author of the story of our life, and in that role there is no possible competitor. We relax. We aren't selling anything. We are offering a gift. Helping people shift from making a case for something to telling their story creates an entirely different response on the listeners' part.

This practice helps people grasp the importance of respecting the perspective of the other, even if that perspective is different from our own. It helps people develop an authentic appreciation for each other. And it helps us all remember that in almost any circumstance there are a variety of perspectives that differ from one another and are critical to a full understanding of the situation.

The MetaSkills Wheel

Another powerful tool which can be used with either individuals or groups is the MetaSkills Wheel. First developed by CRR Global,[1] a relationship systems training organization, this tool is now used worldwide. The purpose of the Wheel is to help people shift their attitudes, stances, and feelings, and the context through which they are viewing any issue or situation. It supports them in shifts of awareness that open possibilities for individuals and teams. The process is best explained by the visual in Figure 6.1 and the following story:

An executive was anticipating a difficult meeting with his business partner. He felt that his partner had profoundly wronged him and his instinct was to go into the meeting and give the man a piece of his mind, to head into the discussion like an oncoming locomotive.

FIGURE 6.1 The MetaSkills Wheel

SOURCE: CCR Global

NOTE: The MetaSkills Wheel is a component of CRR *Global's Organization & Relationship Systems Coaching* curriculum.

Instead, before the meeting, he chose to walk through the MetaSkills Wheel that was marked out with masking tape on a large area of the floor of a meeting room. The wheel named various stances from which to view the dynamic that was troubling him. Walking through the physical dimensions of the wheel added to the power of his experience. As he walked around it, he walked through alternative attitudes and thought processes.

He practiced shifting his stance about the situation, and realized that he could consciously choose the stance that would serve him best in the meeting. The process of the MetaSkills Wheel put his attention on his own interior attitude or outlook rather than on what he would do or say in the meeting. It took him back to the level of beliefs (see Chapter 3), which is part of the groundwork of practices. As he walked, he considered the situation with his business partner from a number of stances, forcing himself to stand a minute or so in each place in order to really "get" the feel of that spot. First he stood in the place of a deep commitment to the relationship, next in a sense of playfulness, then successively in an open heart, a feeling of collaboration, a place of inquiry, openness to all perspectives, and finally a sense of deep respect. As he considered the situation from each of these places, his anger gradually subsided. He then consciously opted for an open heart as the stance he wanted to take in the meeting with his business partner. Starting from this place, he envisioned a whole new approach to their discussion, an approach that met with much success. Many years later he reported that had he not taken the time to do this work beforehand, the meeting would have been disastrous. He felt his life would have been much different without it.

The MetaSkills Wheel reminds us that most of the time when we face challenges in our work and our relationships, we tend to ask ourselves, "What else can I do to get a different result?" Our focus is on *doing*, and we hope we can modify our results through focusing on actions and content. We miss the enormous possibility for breakthrough—for contributing to flourishing teams and organizations—that is possible when we examine (and adjust) the assumptions, frameworks, and context we are holding internally as we are doing whatever we are doing. When we shift how we are seeing whatever is challenging us—and in so doing, who we are *being*—we create new possibilities. We see how the limitations of the way we are holding what is happening have served to create the very reality that is unfolding.

A parallel process from the Oneida Native American culture is the "rule of six," which invites us to come up with six possible, plausible reasons that something might be occurring. Paula Underwood Spencer, an Oneida historian and elder who taught executives this process, said that you could step through the process in a logical, linear, one-step-at-a-time way, or you could sketch six stories, a much more fluid storytelling process.[2] Keeping our mind open to six possibilities and continuing to learn produces an organizational practice that leads to flourishing. Decisions are made after considering a wide range of perspectives and stakeholders.

Such processes help both individuals and groups shift how they are *being* toward a challenge, and in the process they usually find themselves and the situation transformed. The physical experience of processes like walking through the Wheel remind us of the power of physical processes. The body has its own way of remembering what is important. It is this awareness of the body's wisdom that has drawn practitioners like Wendy Palmer and Richard Moon to use practices from the martial art of Aikido to create new understandings about organizational life. Similar knowing is at the heart of the work of Arawana Hayashi, who partners with Otto Scharmer through the Presencing Institute, as well as the work of dancer Liz Lerman, who works with leaders to help instill in them a greater physical awareness.[3] Physical practices such as the MetaSkills Wheel can be powerful reflective practices, reconnecting us with our bodies and drawing our physical ways of knowing into the process.

Jazz Improvisation

Numerous books have been written on the theme of jazz as a metaphor for an organization that is creative and fluid—Max De Pree's *Leadership Jazz*, for instance, and Frank Barrett's *Yes to the Mess: Surprising Leadership Lessons from Jazz.*[4] The metaphors of music of all kinds, but particularly of jazz, are powerful and can open an important conversation that would otherwise not occur.

We offer a story about the power of music performance for understanding organizational problems. It is a story that highlights the power of music and an innovative manufacturing leader who saw the potential in creating a new process on the spot.

One of us was part of a working group helping a manufacturing client design an off-site meeting for the leadership of the fifty-two manufacturing plants worldwide for which he was responsible for quality. He was worried that the plants' defective parts per million were higher than the single-figure target he had set and that he believed was essential to the firm's competitiveness as well as to its cost targets. Things weren't looking so good.

He was frustrated that he couldn't get the leadership of those plants to understand the importance of what he called a cadence, an essential rhythm to manufacturing, a pace, a meter that creates conditions for a higher level of quality. "They just don't seem to get the cadence," he said, slapping one out on the top of the conference table to make his point. "And if they get it, they lose it and can't get it back."

Without censoring her thinking, the off-site facilitator looked at him and said, "Jazz band." "Hire one," he said. So she hired a jazz band for the off-site. The manufacturing executive rehearsed the band and coached them to first play well and then (much to their dismay) to "lose it," that is, to nose into what they called a "train wreck," and then to pull out of it. The group of quite fine university musicians found it hard to believe that they were to play badly when they could play so well, but they were willing to give it a try.

The next day at the off-site, the jazz band was the surprise. Two hundred and fifty manufacturing leaders from around the world sat at round tables through the morning sessions of stats on quality, and listened with interest, and probably some skepticism, to some examples of things going well in some of the plants and to how the leaders had gotten those good results.

Then the manufacturing leader welcomed the band on stage and invited everyone to take a lesson from jazz. He instructed them to listen to the musicians to see what they could learn. He was curious about what they might observe about the process of shared leadership. He wondered what they would notice when the band began to "lose it." He hoped they would pay particular attention to what happened when the musicians began to pull themselves out of what jazz musicians call a "train wreck"—a fairly graphic term for what was happening in some of the company's plants. But the plants often couldn't pull out of the train wreck like the jazz band could. And the question he hoped everyone would begin to ask was, how did the jazz band do it?

The band began to play. Everyone listened and watched. They played well, and then slowly went into the "train wreck," losing the cadence and the thread of the theme. Then they pulled themselves back on track. The manufacturing leader asked them to do it again, and everyone listened.

Then the 250 people in the room engaged in a dialogue. The facilitator asked how many folks played an instrument themselves. Many hands went up. She was surprised. It was an engineering crowd and she hadn't expected so many musicians. "And how many of you have family members or close friends who are serious musicians?" she asked. More hands went up than before. Interesting. " How many of you enjoy music?" Almost all of the hands went up.

"So what did you see when the band played?" All over the room, hands went up.

"I heard the way the theme got set, and then passed from one person to another."

"I could see how the leader could step back and the process just did its own work."

"I heard how the cadence stayed the same."

"I got to thinking about how much they must have practiced individually to get this good."

"And they must have practiced together a lot too."

"I could see how much fun they were having."

"It looked like such fun."

"It looked so easy when it was working."

"And what about the train wreck?" she asked. "What did you see there?"

"Well, at first I couldn't even hear when they were getting off track, but I could see them looking toward each other for the first time, like they were checking on something."

Listen (inside and outside) for information, not confirmation. Set aside judgments of yourself and others. Suspend your assumptions and consider that alternative ones might be more useful. Notice what is surprising to you. Give up your need to hear what you agree with or what you expect. Listen with interest, curiosity.

Allow for silence. Silence can be productive. It may mean people are thinking, considering, taking in what has been said.

Listen generously. Assume that ideas, observations, and stories all come from a desire to contribute. Consider that ideas build on one another, even if you can't see how they hook logically together.

Seek and welcome difference. Remember that difference of opinion can be helpful because it sharpens our collective understanding. Let it be—without debate and without rushing in to smooth things over.

Speak with your fresh voice. Resist the need to say what you usually say. Sit in silence until you find yourself moved to say something that is truly of the moment, in this particular conversation. Remember that listening and waiting to speak are not the same thing. *Speak one person at a time, without interruption.* And think twice before speaking more than once. This is a time to share the airspace.

Bring 100 percent of yourself and allow for 100 percent of the other. Allow for the wisdom of what at first seems irrelevant, in you, and in others.

Bring the gift of your complete attention and presence. Set aside all distractions, internal and external, and give your full attention to this dialogue, here and now.

For a leader who wishes to convene a dialogue, spelling out these skills and approaches in advance helps. Practicing them oneself is essential, as is creating a welcoming context, setting a time limit ("we have about an hour to explore our individual and collective thinking about . . . "), posing or posting a question that invites everyone into the game—for example, "What should be uppermost in our minds as we move forward in this initiative?"—and making clear that this is a time to learn with and from each other, and that there is no intent to make a decision in this one hour—indeed, one might even say, "the decision may not be made until next month, and the board will be the decider. But our conversation today can provide rich and important insights to them."

In one case, dialogue was used to surface a difficult conversation in the telecommunications industry among corporate and labor leaders tangled in a complete impasse over some key issues that lay outside the formal bargaining process. Forty contentious people sat around a large hotel table. One of the leaders initiated a process that created the one-at-a-time listening that is essential to dialogue. He grabbed a KOOSH Ball (a toy ball made of rubber filaments) that the facilitator had on the table and said, "As long as I have this, I have the floor. Let me tell you what is on my mind." He finished quickly, looked around the table for a hand up of whoever wanted to go next, then tossed the KOOSH Ball to that person, who spoke briefly without being interrupted. That person then looked around and tossed the ball to another person who had her hand up. Using such a simple process, the group self-managed an increasingly civil and constructive dialogue for an hour without the facilitator needing to do a thing. In many North American indigenous traditions, the item passed is a "talking stick." In business tradition, anything that signals who has the floor without interruption will do. This practice promotes deep listening, and it breaks our habitual interrupting of one another.

Music performances, whether live or on video, can offer memorable experiences of the power of dialogue. Otto Scharmer often plays a segment of the *Original Three Tenor's Concert* video in which Placido Domingo sings, with Zubin Mehta conducting the orchestra. The video segment helps people see the powerful nonverbal connection and seamless shared leadership in the performance of the two men.

Another example of using music as a prompt to dialogue is the work of Canadian composer and pianist Michael Jones, who, in helping people understand the difference between fixed thinking and fresh thinking, begins by playing a piece he has recorded and for which he is known. Midway through that piece, he subtly shifts to composing a new piece in the moment. Repeating that process, he invites people to see if they can sense the shift from the practiced or "known" composition to the fresh notes. He offers this as an analogy to being able to speak freshly, not from our usual "script," in a dialogue. As people are able to pick up on the difference, he invites them to reflect on when they are able to speak from such a fresh and unrehearsed place within themselves. The tenor of the dialogue changes.

Shared Values Management

Michele Hunt, a board member at the Fowler Center and former Vice President for People at Herman Miller, a furniture design firm, tells the story of the dialogue process they use to align values and business practices, an experience that underscores that a corporation can both *do good* and *do well*. Michele had just begun her vice president role at Herman Miller when the firm ran into trouble. Rapid growth had resulted in many of the company's founding values being left behind. Max De Pree, CEO and chairman of the company, called for "renewal" and gave the leadership team the mandate to engage and involve every person in the company, working in teams, to identify the company's core values. The process the leadership team designed invited everyone to come to a *shared* agreement on the values that Herman Miller should embrace in order to renew their people, their culture, and the business. One key was the quality of their dialogue, which was the result of practice.

Peter Senge initially coached the executive team in the art of dialogue, and a colleague of his conducted off-site retreats over several months involving ninety-six executives and managers who met in groups of twenty-four to explore the company's core values. Much of the dialogue work was reflective and personal—rich conversations about what really mattered to people and to the firm. These ninety-six leaders then engaged their teams in thoughtful conversation to identify key values. Every team in the company participated. A robust, transparent communications system was designed to keep everyone informed and to cheer people along. Through the ongoing dialogue and engagement, the leadership and people of Herman Miller came to shared agreement on seven values:

1. *Customer-focused vision:* See our work through the eyes of our customers.

2. *Participation and teamwork:* Recognize the individual and collective genius in people.

3. *Ownership:* Understand that participation engenders shared ownership for the company's success.

4. *Valuing uniqueness:* Encourage people to bring their whole selves to work and to contribute their uniqueness to help achieve the company's goals. Value and celebrate diversity.

5. *Family social and environmental responsibility:* Work, family, communities, and the environment are inextricably connected; management decisions should aim for innovative solutions that support these critical stakeholders.

6. *Learning organization:* Invest in developing employees, leaders, and teams. Continual learning is a shared responsibility.

7. *Financial soundness:* This is essential but it is not the single aim of our work. It is the result of our commitment to our vision, values, and goals and our collective efforts.

The harder work came next. The leadership team worked with employees to align Herman Miller's policies, processes, structures, and systems with its vision and values. The most important part of the process became the authentic participation of the people at every level of the organization. Leadership created cross-functional, cross-level action teams to make recommendations on how to close the gap between the vision and values they had collectively created and the current reality. The collective commitment of the people of Herman Miller to this participative process yielded remarkable results:

Named *Fortune* magazine's Most Admired Company in America for Social Responsibility 2012

Listed five times as one of *Fortune* magazine Top 100 Best Companies to Work for

Designated Best Company for Women

Named a *Working Mother* magazine Best Company for working mothers

Received numerous environmental awards, including:

White House Presidential citation for environmental management

Fortune magazine list of 10 most environmentally responsible corporations

Cited for Best Products by *Business Week*

Selected Best Managed Company in the world by the Bertelsmann Foundation

Increased sales 20 percent in one year and returned to double digit growth

Experienced two stock splits over the next three years

By using dialogue to surface key values at Herman Miller, the company's leaders were able to create authentic and wholehearted organizational alignment. Their experience underscores the value of individuals strengthening their dialogue skills as a first step in this shared-values process. It points to the importance of creating a context or designing a setting in which dialogue can unfold.

Like Michele Hunt, many of the leaders we interviewed under-scored working with values as a natural path into spiritual dimensions of organizational life. We turn now to such additional values-based practices for organizations wishing to explore spirituality as a path-way to flourishing.

Barrett Cultural Values Assessment

The Barrett Cultural Values Assessment is a reflective practice that allows business leaders to measure and manage their organization-al values.[6] Derived from Abraham Maslow's hierarchy of human needs, the assessment is conducted at seven levels, all necessary for a healthy business culture in which everyone is contributing. The first three levels (Survival, Relationship, and Self-Esteem) are about caring for one's own needs. Level 4 (Transformation) focuses on continuous renewal, learning, empowerment, innovation, and lead-ership development and is a bridge to levels 5, 6, and 7 (Internal Cohesion, Making a Difference, and Service). The last three levels have to do with finding meaning and caring for societal needs. As an organization measures and manages its values on these seven levels, there is a reduction in wasted effort and an improvement in financial performance.

THE PROCESS IN A NUTSHELL

All employees complete a twenty-minute survey anonymously. Each employee answers three questions about a list of values:

a. Which of the following values/behaviors most represent who you are?

b. Which of the following values/behaviors most represent how your organization operates?

c. Which of the following values/ behaviors most represent how you would like your organization to operate?

The Barrett Center provides the organization with a detailed report on the top ten values in each of the three categories (personal, current organization, desired organization) plotted on the seven levels listed earlier. The data can be broken down for relevant subgroups. The process provides a chance for learning and dialogue about potentially limiting values and the positive change that would provide more of the values for which people are asking.

The next work involves aligning values with vision, mission, and the structures of the organization to ensure whole-group cohesion and the capacity for collective action.

Repeating this survey and alignment process every year or so can produce consistent effective change as the organization listens to what people care about and builds a culture that reflects their values, particularly their aspiration for finding meaning in their work. The process also helps people become naturally more conscious of their organization's values. Integrating some of the reflective practices (journaling, dialogue, listening) into the process will further deepen engagement with vision, mission, and values. As this organizational practice repeats over time, the company's ability to contribute to a flourishing society will expand.

One firm was engaged in a company-wide assessment to determine people's personal values, their views of the values currently guiding the firm's behavior, and the desired values necessary for future success. Five of the top ten desired culture values landed in level 4, indicating a strong organizational commitment to transformation. The CEO spoke to that commitment consistently in his messages to his managers as they used the data to determine the three values— teamwork, accountability, and personal growth—saying, "Take care of business every day, but put your attention on our three most important values before you think about going after the next million dollars of revenue."

Over just a few months, this leadership message about "values first," and the managers' focus on living up to these values, yielded two outcomes: a record-breaking revenue month and many expressions of gratitude from both long-term and new employees at the annual all-company meeting. People spoke of being "thrilled about being unified" and "blown away by the idea that the CEO cares about personal growth." They noted that the "connection among our people gives us an advantage over our competition." One new employee stood up at the end of the meeting and said, "I expected a few minutes of rah-rah and pom-poms before we focused on the numbers and market share. What I got was a sincere, emotional experience of our leaders giving a damn. The only thing I can say is, 'Wow, I've never worked anywhere like this before.'" The alignment left people feeling that they could bring their full selves to work.

To put the value of all of this into perspective: a 2013 Gallup poll highlighted by the *Wall Street Journal* estimated that disconnected, unmotivated employees cost the United States $450–$550 billion a year due to high absenteeism and turnover, quality-control issues, and lost productivity.[7]

By matching its perceived current values with its desired values, an organization can identify where to focus improvement efforts with each repeated assessment. Over time the organizational practice of regularly assessing values and improving alignment between existing and desired values produces visible results: it moves a business from being focused only on shareholders to being oriented to a full range of stakeholders, and ultimately to increasing its likelihood of becoming an agent of world benefit.[8] It leaves employees feeling as if they are thriving and contributing to a flourishing organization.

As we explored team and organizational practices, we laid the foundation for practices that support and reinforce the flourishing of systems (including global systems). How does a systems practice build on the reflective practices described so far? How can these practices be further aimed at the 150-year-goal of humans and all life flourishing on the earth forever?

CHAPTER 7

Systems-Level Practices

Now we turn to reflective practices that foster flourishing at the systems level. The systems level encompasses multiple organizations and their stakeholders. The purpose of a systems-level practice is to open up new possibilities for flourishing across an entire industry, and even across multiple sectors of the economy and society—in search of greater world impact.

Systems-level practices build on the individual- and organization-level practices described in the previous two chapters by incorporating them into a larger systems dynamic. An example of a particularly powerful approach to a systems-level practice is the Appreciative Inquiry (AI) Summit enriched with reflective practices to create what we call a W-Holistic AI Summit[1] (discussed in detail later in this chapter). You will see the ways in which the W-Holistic AI Summit methodology builds on the familiar bedrock of some of the individual and team practices described earlier.

The AI Summit, and a tangible illustration of how it can serve flourishing, is highlighted in this chapter, yet the process of weaving reflective practices into a credible change model can be applied to a range of systems-level change frameworks, particularly those in which disciplined ongoing deep engagement is critical. The case we describe here provides information to help business leaders who initiate and lead systems change efforts, as well as background for line executives and others who simply want to know more about the process.

Let's begin with some history and a look at the array of processes and tools that have typically been used for systems change in sustainability initiatives.

Traditional Systems-Level Approaches to Sustainability

The sustainability movement has developed a range of solid analytical processes and tools for plotting strategy at a systems level. Few of these have included any deliberate space for the reflective practices that would increase ongoing engagement for those involved in the effort. We begin by detailing these existing tools so that we can show more clearly how to splice in reflective practices.

The standard systems sustainability toolbox consists of, among other things:

Life-cycle and related analyses: For understanding environmental impacts along the entire value chain (an organization's supply chain, its own operations, and its products and customer solutions).

Eco-efficiency programs: For reducing waste, energy usage, and consumption of other resources such as water within an organization's own operations. These programs are generally designed to reduce both impacts and costs and are often integrated with other cost-saving programs through tools such as Six Sigma, total quality, and process redesign.

Clean energy initiatives: For generating energy on-site or contributing funding to large-scale wind and other projects through the purchase of renewable energy certificates or similar mechanisms. Businesses often incur moderate costs for such programs, but there is additional value in their public relations power, as well as in responding to criticism from environmental organizations such as Greenpeace.

Sustainable supply chain initiatives. To guide purchasing policies, factory standards, inspections and rating systems, and sometimes joint process improvement programs focused on energy, waste, hazards, eco-efficiency, working conditions, and worker health and safety.

Design for Environment (DfE) and environmental solutions initiatives: For achieving energy and eco-efficiency in products and

services by undertaking solutions, such as GE's Ecomagination initiative, that focus on environmentally friendly products and services.

What appear to be missing from this mix of analytic tools are processes that create a sustained emotional connection to the sustainability activities and goals undertaken. As a result, enthusiasm often
fades after a brief experience with environmental and social action.
It's that waning enthusiasm that we aim to turn around.

The loss of enthusiasm happens for good and understandably human reasons. Many sustainability initiatives suffer from becoming
"one more thing to do" in an already overloaded agenda. Complexity and overwhelming workloads are a common challenge for people
working in businesses and institutional systems. For those who are
tackling system-wide sustainability issues, there is an additional problem: because the "cause" is so complex and so compelling, it often
seems impossible to step back and reassess what really works. We
keep soldiering on. The answer always seems to lie in working harder,
working longer hours, working weekends. The cause demands it.

Yet the real resource may lie in working in a different way—in
what leadership expert Peter Vaill calls working *reflectively* smarter,
collectively smarter, and *spiritually* smarter.[2] When integrated into
the systems approach, reflective practices can create those other ways
of working, leading to more lasting connection and commitment.

Those other ways of working are evident in the efforts of German
economist Otto Scharmer in his book *Theory U,* which presents a
system-change process based on the concept of *presencing.* A blend
of the words *presence* and *sensing,* the presencing process creates a
heightened state of attention that allows individuals and groups to
shift the inner place from which they think and act so that they are
operating from a more powerful stance. It uses a number of reflective practices and it is the cumulative impact of those practices that
moves people toward letting go of old ways of being and doing, thus
opening them to a fresher sense of reality and a stronger connection to

an emerging future. Scharmer's process, widely respected in business circles, underscores the importance of empathy, of opening people's hearts as they strengthen their capacity to listen, to expand their awareness, and to move toward what Scharmer calls a field of inspired connections. He suggests seven factors that support that movement and help in making those connections. We include them here to indicate their importance for any sustained systems-level change effort.

1. A shared desire to innovate among the senior leaders of the participating institutions

2. A diverse microcosm of players that mirrors the key stakeholders of the larger whole

3. Dialogue with inspired, remarkable people who have changed the system

4. Deep-dive sensing journeys that take the group to the edges of a system, where they can experience its marginalized stakeholders

5. Stillness and deep reflection practices that allow people to connect to the source of inner knowing and to the profound journey of discovering who they really are and what they are here for

6. Rapid-cycle prototyping projects that provide safe practice fields in which to link the intelligence of the head, heart, and hands

7. A support infrastructure that helps to move projects with the best results from the prototyping stage into the next stage of institutional innovation

We can see in these factors many of the same ones we described in Chapter 5 as part of the system immersion experience designed for Lee Scott at Walmart.

In presencing as in other widely regarded change approaches such as Marvin Weisbord's Future Search and the World Café method,[3] we see that the first step to improving existing strategic, organizational, and operational sustainability efforts lies in incorporating reflective practices such as those described in Chapters 5 and 6. Such practices don't require more work at the system-change level; they simply change *how* we do that work. They increase people's connection to the work and to each other.

We have incorporated some key reflective practices along with the powerful systems process of Appreciative Inquiry to produce what we call W-Holistic Appreciative Inquiry, so named because it focuses us on the whole human being and the whole system. W-Holistic AI is an enhancement of the well-known process of Appreciative Inquiry. To understand the innovation of W-Holistic AI, as well as the appreciative orientation of AI (which turns out to be a key orientation), we need to get the basics of AI itself, so fasten your seatbelts as we move quickly through this rich material.

Appreciative Inquiry is a whole-system change methodology with a global following that focuses on the positive (strength-based) dimensions of an organization within its larger system. In providing an affirmative process for accessing and building on the strengths of a system, it broadens people's capacity to engage in change.

David Cooperrider, whose name is most prominently associated with AI, has identified three assumptions that support an affirmative basis of organizing.[4] His first assumption is that organizations are products of affirmative minds. This assumption acknowledges the human capacity to project ahead a horizon of expectations that brings the future powerfully into the present as a causal agent.[5] The second assumption is that, when beset with stubborn difficulties or problems, organizations and systems need less fixing, less problem-solving, and more reaffirmation—or more precisely, greater appreciation of what it is like to succeed. That is, they should learn from their own success. The third assumption is that the primary executive vocation is nourishing the appreciative soil in which innovation, creativity, and breakthroughs grow. It is the soil that nourishes flourishing within an organization, for this is where positive guiding images grow on a collective and dynamic basis. In the process of nourishing the appreciative soil, an executive can become the kind of leader for whom most of us long to work—a leader who is capable of recognizing and using his or her strengths, supporting teamwork, and accomplishing the task at hand. In this world, a leader's job is to bring out the best in people. Appreciative Inquiry facilitator Connie Fuller reminds us that AI distinguishes itself from traditional organizational development change methodologies by virtue of its optimistic assumptions about people, organizations, and relationships. (To the cynics among us we would say, the optimistic assumptions may not always be warranted, but they are always powerful.)

Appreciative Inquiry has evolved extensively since the mid-1980s. Thousands of enterprises and institutional systems worldwide have embraced AI in order to foster systematic and transformative change. Networks of practitioners and scholars are active on several continents to share, refine, and evolve its practice and theory. AI enables keen insight into multiple stakeholder perspectives, allows strong relationships to be built, and stimulates extraordinary levels of creativity, innovation, and collective intelligence. Importantly, it enables aligned action, even among constituencies who have a history of confrontation and counterproductive relations.

Over the past decade, research findings in positive organization science and positive psychology have helped us better understand the mechanisms that produce AI's fast and powerful results. Of particular note is the work of Marcial Losada with Emily Heaphy and later Barbara Fredrickson, which we described in Chapter 6 and which points to the drivers of team performance. Losada and his coauthors identified positive dialogue and inquiry as the two key attributes that distinguish high- from low-performing teams. AI, by design, creates conditions for positive dialogue and inquiry such that the conversations in the room result in more constructive and creative dialogue, thereby moving the group to higher performance.

The basic principles of AI (many of which underlie the individual and organizational practices presented in chapters 5 and 6) are also evident in its evolution, which we detail here because that evolution gives important clues to the various scales and purposes for which AI can be used:

Stage I. *1986: AI as a strengths-based approach for change.* The early work was aimed at planting, within individuals and organizations, the idea that effective change requires focusing on strengths rather than weaknesses, on assets rather than liabilities. It initiates the process of orienting change initiatives to the strengths of a person (or a system) and away from what is wrong with them (or it). From early on, the purpose of AI has been to help organizations move from deficit-based thinking to possibility-seeking. The process begins with a question about peak experiences within an organization, posed to individuals in the organization. For example: "Tell us about a time when you were at your very best at work?" One of the expected outcomes of the first stage of AI is greater commitment to and engagement within a system.

Stage II. *1990s: AI Summits for whole-system dialogue.* This stage created the capacity for dialogue across multiple stakeholders and demonstrated its power across a broad array of systems. Leveraging the early success of AI, the purpose of an AI Summit is to promote dialogue among multiple stakeholders representing the whole system in order to generate system-wide results. The outcome: everyone feels a sense of belonging to the larger system and has a greater sense of ownership of its path forward.

Stage III. *2000s: Appreciative Inquiry Process for Sustainability.* Now we can see the beginning of the focus on using AI for sustainability. As the AI model matured, its focus on possibility-seeking became a focus on business as a force for good, as an agent for world benefit. In this phase, AI practitioners sought to expand the role of business in society by sharing success stories in which business has played just such a role.

Stage IV. *2010s: W-Holistic Appreciative Inquiry.* We see at this stage
the intentional inclusion of the spiritual dimension, the reflective
practices interwoven throughout the 4-D (Discovery, Dream,
Design, Destiny) cycle shown in Figure 7.1.

The cycle represents a powering-up of AI by tapping into the
reflective-spiritual dimension while focusing system change on the
goal of flourishing.

Building on experience with business as an agent of world benefit,
the work done at an AI Summit weaves individual and small-group
reflective practices into the overall AI fabric, thus promoting connection in the sense discussed in earlier chapters. This has allowed AI
practice to aim more directly at the goal of flourishing.

AI and Sustainability: The Dairy Industry Case

What does an AI Summit look like? We turn to an example from the
dairy industry that can be seen as a system involving everyone from
the cow to the consumer. You can think of this case as a Stage III
Appreciative Inquiry process in which the dairy industry took the
AI Summit process, with its inclusiveness and connection-making,
and focused it on the challenges of sustainability in order to reduce
greenhouse gases. In doing so, they were aware that before any AI
Summit it is essential to perform additional upfront analysis and
framing in order to identify and inform stakeholders who are most
critical to the eventual success of a specific improvement effort. They
needed to include players who would be part of any emergent system
and who would need to be committed to implementing the associated breakthrough solutions—as well as those who were part of the
current system.

The three-day summit, which was convened to explore greenhouse gas (GHG) reduction opportunities in the U.S. fluid milk value
chain, drew 250 people from all parts of the value chain—from feed
production and farming through retail—in order to include a broad
range of industry stakeholders.

SYSTEMS-LEVEL PRACTICES   131

This is what members of a system learn about AI Summit as they begin the process: The AI Summit convenes a whole system of internal and external strengths in a concentrated way to plan, design, and implement around a topic of strategic importance. Moreover, the summit provides an opportunity for everyone to be engaged as a designer, across all relevant and resource-rich boundaries, to share leadership and take ownership for making the future of a key opportunity successful.

The summit is based on the notion that the power of the whole brings out the best in strength-based management and in human systems. The results occur faster, more consistently, and more effectively than in any other approach. The summit fosters creativity and innovation by focusing on strengths consistent with the leadership philosophy articulated by Peter Drucker: "the essential task of leadership is to create an alignment of strengths in ways that make a system's weaknesses irrelevant."[6] It emphasizes managing and leading change from strengths: elevating strengths, magnifying strengths, and creating new combinations and chemistries of strengths that propel innovation.

A multi-stakeholder steering team leads and prepares for the summit by

Framing the summit task

Conducting and summarizing pre-summit analysis in order to provide common context and insight about the current system and possible futures

Inviting and enrolling participants representing all parts of the system

Coordinating system logistics

Laying the foundation for post-summit governance

A summit lasting only three or four days can accomplish what would typically require months. It can achieve results that would otherwise be impossible without full engagement of the whole system.

It is startling how quickly an AI Summit fosters greater trust and strong relationships among diverse constituencies, including parties who have long histories of confrontation. During the summit, stakeholders develop deep mutual understanding, create road maps together, become committed to a common vision, and agree on a set of aligned projects. A properly designed summit rapidly produces creative results and achieves outcomes that are difficult (if not impossible) to achieve by any other method.

The designers of the summit make sure that the participants represent a slice of the whole system that is relevant to the summit topic. There is almost no limit to the number of people who can participate. The best summits anticipate and include all those who will play a key role in implementing the desired change. Such summits may include two hundred, five hundred, or even more than a thousand participants. This number of people may appear cumbersome to those who have not experienced a summit, but it turns out that the opposite is true; because the whole system develops the vision, and the plan, participants are fully engaged and committed to the change ahead.

The AI model for summit structure is based on a theory of positive change, as shown in Figure 7.1. The process begins with the Discovery phase. The purpose of this phase is both to identify the positive core of the system on which the future will be built, and to develop positive and creative relationships among summit participants. This phase starts with choosing a topic, which is defined before the summit. The Summit itself begins with an interview process in which each participant shares with one other participant a personal high-point story about a time when the person was successful regarding the chosen topic, such as leading or engaging in meaningful change. The discussion then expands to all the occupants around tables of eight to twelve people. From there, appreciative discussion focuses on the various strengths that make up the positive core of the organizations and system that are participating in the summit. During this

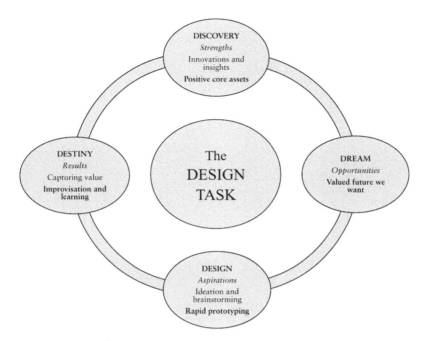

FIGURE 7.1 The 4-D Appreciative Inquiry Process

SOURCE: David Cooperrider, "The Concentration Effect of Strengths: How the Whole System 'AI' Summit Brings Out the Best in Human Enterprise." *Organizational Dynamics*, 41, no. 2, 106–117.

phase it is also helpful to inform participants about the context, the system, and the task through well-designed presentations that provide insightful ways to see and understand the system, its dynamics, and its opportunities. This phase builds the platform of strengths from which the images of the future will emerge.

The second phase of the summit is called Dream. Here the diverse participants around each table develop their own vision of a compelling future. These vision statements are then shared throughout the summit hall and a compelling collective vision emerges that everyone in the room can get behind. The experience of this phase is also quite surprising to people, who are invariably amazed and excited by the bold, creative, and compelling ideas that arise.

In the Design phase, participants identify innovations that will

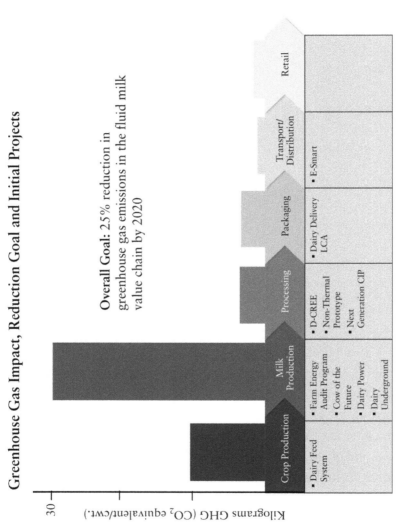

FIGURE 7.2 Dairy Industry GHG Emission Reductions in the Life Cycle Value Chain

SOURCE: Blu Skye Consulting and the Innovation Center for U.S. Dairy. See http://www.usdairy.com/sustainability.

bring the Dream to life. They then vote with their feet and organize around the initiatives they are most passionate about bringing to fruition. The purpose of this phase is to rapidly prototype each innovation through a co-creative process that captures the collective intelligence of the prototype team.

Finally, the Destiny phase (sometimes called the Deploy phase) is used to envision how to move forward from prototype to reality in the world. Typically, one or more teams will design the governance and resourcing structures needed for implementing the plans and tackling the tasks detailed in the previous phase.

The results of the dairy industry's AI Summit are summarized in Figure 7.2, which shows the overall goal and the pilot projects by value-added activity as the outcomes of the summit. The results were also reported in the press: In December 2009, the dairy industry entered into an historic agreement with the federal government—announced at the global climate change summit in Copenhagen—to work together to realize a 25 percent GHG reduction goal. "This historic agreement, the first of its kind, will help us achieve the ambitious goal of drastically reducing greenhouse gas emissions while benefiting dairy farmers."[7]

Since that summit, the collaborative effort in the dairy industry has moved forward in four key areas: research, goals, projects, and measurement and reporting. More than eight hundred team members have participated in industry sustainability efforts, resourced with more than $10 million in cash and in-kind service.[8] Note that these impressive results were achieved before the creation of the even more powerful process of W-Holistic AI Summit, which engenders even more sustained effort because of the inclusion of additional reflective practices. Before we turn to that process, we highlight the business impacts of the foundational AI process, even before the addition of the reflective practices that more fully engage participants over the long haul and increase the depth of their commitment to taking innovative action that will produce the planned outcomes.

Business Value of AI Summits for Systems Change

What has been the response to the AI summit by individuals, organizations, and leaders? And what have been the business results? One example from the United States is Roadway Express, which engaged ten thousand people in sixty-five AI Summits, spawning a culture of twenty-five thousand employees thinking and acting like owners of the business, reducing grievances from three hundred to zero, eliminating the need for a formal grievance process, increasing throughput from 47 percent to 64 percent, and reducing average transit speed from 2.3 to 2.1 days. Over the period of AI Summit implementation, Roadway's stock price rose from $14 to $41 per share. In 2002, a few years after the start of the AI work at Roadway, one of the AI teams came up with a $10 million per year cost-savings idea. Roadway later merged with Yellow to form Yellow Roadway Corporation. As a testimony to the perceived value of the AI change process, the AI Summit was selected as the approach to bring the two organizations together. The synergistic savings from this merger were estimated at $300 million.

Another case in point is the Hunter Douglas Window Fashions Division in Broomfield, Colorado, the leading manufacturer of energy-efficient window coverings in the United States, which used AI to engage employees, customers, suppliers, and community members in generating a new corporate vision and changing the corporate culture to increase productivity and employee commitment. As a result, there was a consistent decline in the company's employee turnover rate in absolute terms and in comparison with turnover statistics for the area marketplace.

Such experiences with the AI Summit have demonstrated the business results that come from a process that acknowledges that people want to be involved and to contribute to change initiatives. They are more than willing to offer their ideas and perspectives regarding what works for them, what they would like to change, and what they would like to keep. AI opens the door to their wholehearted participation while helping them "think outside the box." In these organizations, employees were encouraged to discover what gave life to their organizations and to explore what they would like to keep no matter how much change occurs.

What has delighted executives who have utilized AI is that something extraordinary happens when a whole system is present in a room and people begin to share the best of who they are. They start learning about their own and others' strengths and become aware of the connections between the various parts of the system. They begin to see the system as a whole and recognize the impact they have on each other. It becomes second nature for them to realize that their daily tasks are not isolated from other departments and that the challenges they face are also part of a larger connection. And in such an appreciative environment, dialogue turns into empathetic interaction.

Working within an AI framework, participants from separate parts of a system get acquainted and become committed to helping one another. If they need information, they know where to find it: The experience can help them become increasingly knowledgeable about how the system works and who is responsible for doing what. The participation in decision-making, involvement in strategic planning, and creation of spaces for open dialogue offered by these approaches to change create effective paths that increase employees' sense of belonging and recognition, and their feelings of equality.

Although planning for and leading an AI Summit is a complex task and requires a significant investment of time and energy, organizations with experience in the process increasingly realize the value of having everyone present and operating at their very best, which is what happens when the whole system is represented in a room and engaged in the AI Summit process. Organizations count on employees becoming protagonists who are invested in the system's success. No longer spectators or passive voices in the change process, people will participate in plans for change, try out innovative solutions, and implement and sustain the changes. In short, they will persistently engage in concrete action.

The AI Summit process creates an environment in which people feel comfortable being fully themselves, searching for the best in one another, inquiring into what gives life to others and to the organization, and remembering their own victories. In such an environment, communication among participants becomes rich and authentic. People are excited to share their success stories and are comfortable speaking their truth. Here there is no need to convince one person to agree with another's point of view. There are no prizes for telling the most successful story. There is no competition among life stories. Instead, there is respect for the diversity of images and feelings that accompanied those experiences. This approach values human potential and encourages active participation, and in this way it liberates the human spirit and helps participants take actions that are consistent with their shared image of the future.

W-Holistic AI—
Appreciative Inquiry with Reflective Practice
Given the experience of AI Summits such as that of the dairy industry, we seized the opportunity to increase the impact of such efforts by enriching the process with several forms of reflective practice placed at strategic touchpoints in the process. We intended for those practices to increase participant engagement and provide a more lasting impact and commitment to action on their part. Some AI practitioners, including David Cooperrider, had already been experimenting with integrating reflective practices (such as poetry, art, and meditative silence) into the AI Summit methodology, and were finding that early inclusion of such reflection created a more profound and lasting set of connections. Their experiences spurred us to go further with such innovations.

We prototyped the first AI Summit in which reflective practices were systematically woven into the AI process from beginning to end.

We share the design and results of that prototype with you to encourage you to explore this richer variant of AI Summit. We have found in it explicit support for key reflective elements at each of the four AI stages, producing for the participants a more engaged experience at an AI Summit, but also providing encouragement and support for them to continue using the practices when then return home.

W-Holistic AI purposefully adds to the AI experience of connection and wholeness. The *W* represents wholeness and directs our attention to the urgent need for stakeholders to experience a sense of connection to the larger system of which they are a part; and AI is holistic because it perceives the individual as a living system whose ability to thrive depends on interaction with the whole. We are by no means suggesting that AI is the only large-scale, whole-system change process with the potential to support flourishing. Nor do we claim that the reflective practices we choose to incorporate within it are the only ones capable of raising it to a higher level. We have given prominent attention to AI, although we have also had good experiences with other large-scale change processes, such as Future Search, Presencing, and World Café, in which we have observed reflective practices aimed at a system-wide exploration of sustainability challenges. These experiences in other whole-system change efforts have been in arenas as diverse as the airline industry working to reduce its carbon footprint, and a privately held construction firm creating a more innovative leadership group in order to address sustainability issues. We should note that many AI Summits creatively incorporate practices from those other well-regarded large-scale change processes.

But AI remains, in our estimation, the most promising model for bringing together reflection and flourishing to produce system-level change. AI has already made significant contributions to business success, and many business leaders know it well for its power to foster large-scale change. It has the capacity to compress time and resources, by engaging all the voices in a system in a three-day event instead of the usual small-group work with sequential handoffs that may take many months or even years. The commitment that AI engenders to the work that follows the summit is always impressive.

With the addition of reflective practices—such as poetry, meditation, journaling, music, and time in nature—W-Holistic AI increases opportunities for people to experience not only the wholeness of the system, but also the wholeness of themselves as human beings: It does so because it provides a breathing space for deep reflection during the process.

If the positive orientation of the dialogue at the center of AI helps people to connect to the best of who they are and to imagine the best of what they can become, W-Holistic AI creates an environment in which the heart leads their sense of connection and they learn to value one another at a deep level. It promotes ongoing, sustained actions that arise from a connection to people's deepest source of creativity, which, when applied to the life of the system, will help the system to flourish.

The integration of repeated, specific reflective practices into the standard AI Summit process is shown in Figure 7.3 on page 142. The integration of the subphases (1a, 2a, 3a, 4a, and 4c) of the reflective practices into the traditional AI process is represented by steps on the infinity sign.

A more detailed schema of the design elements in each phase of W-Holistic AI is shown in Table 7.1 on page 143. The reflective exercise preceding each of the four phases has been designed to ready the participants to connect and engage more fully. It is indicated by the *a* added to the numbers corresponding to the phases. For the final phase, Destiny, we've provided an additional *c* element, designed to provide takeaway tools so that people stay connected and committed to the work. Each element is designed to achieve specific outcomes, as shown in the outcomes column. The exercises illustrate the types of reflective practices that can be used to help move people and the system toward desired outcomes.

So here is what W-Holistic AI looks like in action:

W-Holistic AI

The Case of the Federation of Industries of the State of São Paulo, Brazil. Also known as FIESP, this organization is one of the most powerful agents for change in Brazil. FIESP is a membership organization of 132 business associations, representing more than 140,000 companies in the state of São Paulo. It is an affiliate of the National Confederation of Industry of Brazil, a network organized at the state level across the country. Each state-run federation operates on a budget generated through payroll taxes on industry partners to provide a variety of social and business services.

From a non-Brazilian perspective, FIESP is an unusual organization. It is part union, part chamber of commerce, part social service. FIESP engages in lobbying efforts to promote business; it owns and operates a full range of primary, secondary, and technical schools; it runs training programs that serve the employment needs of its industry partners; and it provides health care, child care, and cultural and sports programs for industry partner employees and their families. By reputation, the quality of these operations surpasses those offered by the government, literally touching the lives of millions of people. If there were one organization that could affect social change on a large scale in Brazil, it would be FIESP.

FIESP chose to use a W-Holistic AI Summit framework to disseminate the Millennium Development Goals (MDGs) throughout Brazil. They wanted to mobilize the state's industries to implement actions aligned with the MDGs that provide directions to assist nations seeking to improve the quality of human development and reduce poverty. The organizers saw that for the launch of what was to be an ongoing engagement process, AI could create a culture of active participation as part of the effort to achieve the MDGs. We saw this as an opportunity to prototype W-Holistic AI.

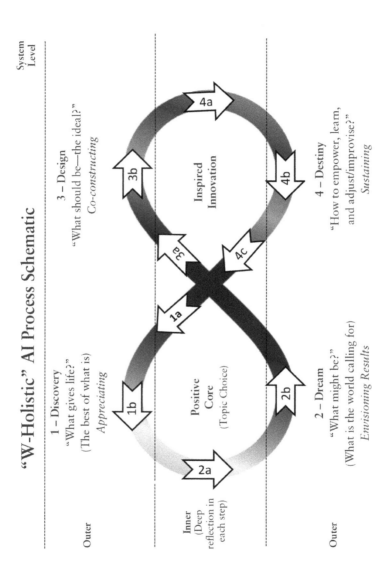

FIGURE 7.3 The 4-D Cycle of Appreciative Inquiry with Reflective Practices
SOURCE: Used with permission of *The Journal of Corporate Citizenship.*

TABLE 7.1 Reflective Exercises (Steps 1a–4a plus 4c) in the AI Summit Process

Phase	Step	Outcomes	Exercises
Discovery	1a	**Connection** – Readiness to experience connection through wholeness within ourselves, with others, with the planet, and with the oneness of all that is	• **Reflection:** *A poem or quote, breathing, and/or silent reflection (5–10 minutes)* • **Letting Go of Judgment and Deep Listening:** *Open mind, empathetic and connected listening (preferred, 1 hour)*
	1b	Collective appreciation of positive core of the organization/system	• Traditional AI Step 1 collective process
Dream	2a	**Calling** – Discovering the boundless meaning for your life and work and for this project	• **Highest Goal:** *What is my highest goal, "what I live for," and how do I need to be to bring it into the future we are creating?*
	2b	Collective vision for organization/system that encompasses individual purposes	• Traditional AI Step 2 process
Design	3a	**Creative Source** – Access the source of deepest creativity and make it available to realize our dream	• **Creative Source:** *Experiential exercise in which participants get in touch with a moment when creativity flowed, either in their childhood or at some other time. Feel and draw the experience on a piece of paper. (20 minutes)*
	3b	Unified architecture of key elements in the collective vision	• Traditional AI Step 3 process
Destiny	4a	**Values in Action** – Thoughtful behavior that reflects the inner states of connection, calling, and creative source	• **Ways of Being and Ways of Doing Dialogue:** *(15 minutes)* • **Values in Action:** *Who do I need to be and how do I need to be different to realize this dream? (20 minutes)*
	4b	Values, structures, and processes for bringing the vision to fruition	• Traditional AI Step 4 process
	4c	**Flourishing Toolbox** – Introduction of toolbox for flourishing process that includes deeper exploration of connection, calling, creative source, values in action, and spiritual resilience	• **Toolbox:** *Introductory presentation (including live-withs) that can be used with tele-calls (minimum 10 minutes)* • **Transformational Problem Solving** *and one other practice from the toolbox (preferred, 2 hours)*

SOURCE: Used with permission of the *Journal of Corporate Citizenship*.

NOTE: Italics denote additions to traditional AI approach.

D1: DISCOVERY

We invited participants onto the journey by asking them to practice connecting to the best of their pasts and to shed light on moments when they felt truly extraordinary. We introduced the AI concept and followed that introduction with a discussion of the importance of deep listening, because they would be sharing stories with each other later that morning. To clarify what we meant by deep listening, we showed the YouTube video of Placido Domingo to which we alluded in Chapter 6, in which he and conductor Zubin Mehta were able to engage fully with each other from their hearts.[9] Scharmer uses this video to highlight the importance of deeper levels of listening in his Presencing Foundation Program. It provides an example of a profound connection between two skilled individuals resulting from focused and respectful listening. We then asked participants to think of a time when they had listened equally deeply and were so in tune with someone else that they could sense what the other person was about to say. They then jotted down some notes about these experiences and were asked to keep them for later use.

The difference between the Discovery phase of this AI Summit and those of other summits was that people engaged in the Discovery process with a completely new mindset and way of being. They were more present and connected with others and seemed able to feel a deeper empathy. During the paired interviews that are a standard part of the beginning of this process, we could measure the impact of their earlier reflective work on the quality of the outcomes at this stage. Our facilitator also reported feeling a sense of oneness and connectedness with the participants at a level she had never experienced before.

The next day, to our surprise, there were more than 170 people in the room, although initially only 120 had been invited to the event. This was far more people than on day one. At first we couldn't figure out what had happened. Later we learned that people had called their colleagues to come because of the powerful experience of the day before.

We began the second day with five minutes of awareness meditation. We asked participants to sit on their chairs with their backs straight and concentrate on their breathing. This activity created a calm spirit in the room as we continued with the traditional AI Discovery phase, during which participants shared with each other their appreciative high-point stories from the notes they'd taken the day before and together uncovered the positive core.

D2: DREAM

In the W-Holistic AI process we have discovered that the sooner we guide participants to use their intuition to connect to their own life's purpose, the more they will feel part of the organization's or system's purpose. The Dream phase allows us to do that.

We began the Dream phase with an exercise created by Michael Ray: My Highest Goal.[10] We asked everyone present to write their responses to the following questions: *What do I live for? How do I need to be to bring myself into the future we are creating?* In addition we gave them five minutes to write down a few words about their personal goals.

The remainder of the Dream Phase was completed just as it would be in a traditional AI Summit: skits dramatizing the vision of the future were created at each table—emerging this time out of the writing about the highest goal—and people presented them to one another. The impact of the Dream phase of the standard AI Summit process is well known: participants immediately feel highly connected to the collective vision and compelled to act toward implementing it, which is very important for the success of the endeavor. It this case, it was clear that the My Highest Goal exercise had helped participants connect even more deeply to the shared vision, creating an even deeper commitment on their part to realizing that vision.

D3: DESIGN

Before working on designing and prototyping specific initiatives—the Design phase—we inserted two reflective exercises to help everyone access their deepest sources of creativity. The first exercise was to envision the old habits that each person would need to let go of and the new ones they would need to begin in order to achieve the collective vision.

The second exercise was a ten-minute activity called Accessing Deep Creativity. We asked participants to remember a moment when their creativity flowed; it might have been a moment from childhood or from some other time, perhaps when they were a teenager. We asked, *What was the experience? How did you feel? How do you feel now when you remember the experience? How can this experience influence how you work on your designs today?* Then we asked them to write down a few words about the experience. Next we asked them to find a moment filled with emotions from a time in their lives when they felt truly able to create something new. After those brief reflective processes, we noticed that the participants started to co-create initiatives that were aligned with the MDGs purpose to improve the lives of disadvantaged people. Their discourse about actions moved from what "they need to do" to "I and my team will do it!"

D4: DESTINY

We began the Destiny phase by bringing mindfulness into the room—noting that to be mindful is to accept not only one's personal current reality without judgment but also to accept the full range of future possibilities. At this point in the process, such a mindfulness exercise is very important. It becomes a breathing moment during which a person can reconnect to his or her purpose. It can take the form of a guided meditation or a period of reflective journaling. In this case, we chose a reflective journaling exercise. We knew that following the Dream phase of the AI process, participants are extremely excited about their future together. They have developed a clear image of what they want and feel compelled to turn those images into reality. Yet some participants can lose the connection between themselves and the world around them, and perhaps even feel overwhelmed.

A reflective journaling exercise promotes stillness in the room and assists participants as they reconnect to their own thoughts and feelings, thus better situating themselves to enter the next phase of the AI process, the Destiny phase.[11] The steps in this reflective journaling process are as follows:

1. By now familiar with the use of reflective processes at the summit, participants needed a chance to connect to their deep creative capacity. We invited people to think and write about a time in their childhood when they were most creative, and then to share those memories with another person by explaining what had made their creative capacity thrive. What was the environment like? Who else was involved, and what role did that person play in the experience?

2. Then we led them in a process of reflective journaling, much akin to automatic writing. We instructed them not to overthink but to let their hands do the writing in response to the questions we read to them. Our questions took them back to their early creative experience and asked for quick insights:

   a. What three words would describe you in that earlier situation?

   b. What two or three characteristics of the environment allowed you to be so creative?

   c. What three words would describe you now? And your work?

   d. What drains your energy at work? What excites you the most about your work right now?

   The questions continued, turning toward the person's gifts and the dreams they have for themselves and their organization.

3. Armed with the notes from their journal, each person found a partner and went outside (ideally participants go into a natural setting) to share a few highlights of their journaling. They were reminded to decide for themselves what they wanted to share.

We noticed after the reflective journaling session and the pair conversations outside that the participants seemed completely ready to collaborate in the implementation of the collective dream. They were also ready to welcome the various new perspectives that people had acquired on how to achieve it.

Next we turned to a values-in-action activity, in which we asked each person to consider, in a way that resonated deeply with their highest goal, who they needed to be and what they needed to do differently to achieve the shared dream. We asked them to read slowly what they had written in the Dream phase about their highest goal, and then to maintain silence for the next five minutes to reflect on their most important personal values. We explained that these values could support their ultimate goal. We then asked them to remember a difficult situation when they "did the right thing."

The next question was, *What were the values that supported that decision or action?* We asked them to write down the three most important values on which they wanted to focus during the next six months as they worked toward implementing their collective dream. Next to each of those values they were to identify three behaviors that are aligned with their values that they would need in order to face major challenges. They then turned to share those values with the person to their right.

In conclusion, during the experience of this AI Summit, with reflective practices woven into each of the four AI phases, we noticed important differences between what had taken place here and what typically occurs in a conventional AI Summit. There seemed to be at least four ways in which the reflective dimensions of W-Holistic AI brought the usual AI Summit process to a higher level of impact. It enabled participants to do the following:

Be more fully present and connected.

See their own deepest purpose or "highest goal" within the collective vision.

Access a deeper capacity for creativity.

Better tap into their latent power to bring their part of the collective vision to fruition.

The impact on one bystander in particular, the security guard who stood at the back of the room all day at the FIESP summit, was startling. At the end of the first day, he had this to say about what he'd seen:

Security guards are almost invisible; we stand in the back of the room and do our job and, if we wish, we can listen to all kinds of topics and work being presented. But our main job is to make sure that everyone is safe as they enter and exit the room. We are used to speeches and conversations in this room; most of the time we do not necessarily pay attention to what is said. But for me this one was very different. . . . I was drawn into what was going on and something within me changed very deeply."

When asked where and what the shift was for him, he put his hand on his chest, near his heart, and tapped twice: "I am not sure what it was, but it was right here!"

W-Holistic AI provides us with an organic framework within which to change our habits of mind and develop new ones that enable us to be more aware of our existing interconnectedness. It gives us permission to tell more heartfelt stories about our lives and about how we relate to future possibilities. Reflective practices help us to look deeply for new ways to give meaning to our experiences beyond our usual habits of judgment. Such practices help us discover meaning by connecting more traditional hard data analysis with other forms of knowing, such as intuition and paying attention to how the body responds. The W-Holistic AI process provides, within its design, the space needed to realize these other possibilities and to access a deeper level of understanding that comes from our own deep wisdom.

Conclusion on Systems-Level Practices

A variety of high-engagement sustainability change processes (such as Future Search, Presencing, , and World Café) can also be strengthened by including additional reflective practices. But a centerpiece of our exploration of systems-level reflective practice remains Appreciative Inquiry and the variant enriched with reflective practice, which we term W-Holistic AI and which is a particularly powerful blending of a research-based change model with reflective practice in pursuit of flourishing. It is along that path that we are investing our continuing practice and research. We invite others to join us on that path.

CHAPTER 8

Conclusion
The Path Forward

We have walked with you through a new orientation that is needed in order for enterprise to succeed in the years ahead. As a group of individuals long invested in maximizing business performance, we traced how enterprise sustainability efforts have disappointed in both results and meaning. Sustainability, as it has been framed to date, has primarily led to the more limited outcome of doing less harm. Now our efforts need to turn toward a very different goal: that of flourishing, and the proposition that we humans and all other life have the possibility to flourish in the long term. The missing link to that future is a mindset and spirit of interconnected people, organizations, and living systems.

Along the path we have traveled, we have sifted through the vast body of research coming from management, psychology, neuroscience, physics, evolutionary biology, and many other fields, linking enterprise success to organizations in which the whole person is encouraged to show up. We have brought fresh ideas about spirituality and sustainability from in-depth conversations with global thought leaders and executives who are leading in ways that allow their companies to flourish—firms that are doing well because they are actively choosing to do good. With those exemplars in mind, we have created a map for new understanding and action.

The shape of that map includes these ideas: Taken together, spirituality and sustainability (or we should say reflective practices and flourishing) are powerful combinations. They become vital in the complex and interdependent world in which we and our organizations are expected to offer environmental health and social benefits as an integral part of everything we do.

How these ideas can show up in the daily work of individuals, in the efforts of our organizations, and within broader systems that impact sustainability is represented by the reflective practices. Our stories of experiences with leaders and organizations trace subtle shifts and the "aha moments" of executives, teams, and whole systems. The practices aim at inviting the human spirit into work settings, with the belief that without the participation of the human spirit, we have hit a wall. Some practices are suited for individuals alone, and many of those can be used in organizations as well. Others are designed for groups and teams. And still others, such as W-Holistic Appreciative Inquiry, are designed as integrative whole systems processes.

The relatively small set of specific reflective practices that we have offered are just the tip of an iceberg of a vast array of rich resources that can help in the development of flourishing people, organizations, and systems.[1] We are keenly aware that practice must fit context. Context counts. We know that factors other than these practices are enormously influential when it comes to the life of an enterprise taken in its larger context. And there are practices beyond those we have highlighted here that you may be able to bring to this work to further enrich the soil of your organization.

But our beginning point is to focus here and now on the practices that we have found promote individual flourishing as well as flourishing relationships at the organizational and systems levels. We know that life within a specific business or system includes many perceived pressures—the economy, uncertainty, the basic structures, authority dynamics, hierarchies, roles and responsibilities, safety and working conditions, policies, and cultural norms—to name but a few. Those pressures and barriers are not the dominant theme in this narrative. The story we are telling is about the power of connection, caring, and commitment to ultimately reshape those dimensions.

The work of transforming organizations and systems so they may develop the creative solutions the world needs, will demand the engagement of people far beyond a relatively small circle that each of us may see today. Many people are already hard at work on one or another dimension of the challenge before us. Some we can see, others are invisible to us. Still others have yet to engage with or even discover these ideas. Among those we are counting on most are the young people in our business and management schools. For the expanding engagement required to pursue the vision, and to achieve a tipping point for business to act as an agent of world benefit, we need to create a social movement of people who are persistently, doggedly, and enthusiastically committed to moving their organizations and the broader system toward the goal of flourishing.

To us, the stepping stone to such a social movement seems likely to be the engagement of the many leaders within businesses, nongovernmental organizations, and other enterprises for whom this vision resonates. Moving toward it requires various collaborative structures and communities of practice that create gathering places—actual and virtual—where those who share the passion for this work can exchange information, encouragement, experiences, practices, and research. The history of other social change movements suggests that community (or communities) of practice may well be a first step toward such a movement, much as was true in the growing power of the civil rights movement in the twentieth-century United States. We should remember that the courage we then saw in the streets was the result of disciplined learning: the Highlander School in Tennessee served as a place to learn critical practices in nonviolent social change, and to foster what became over time a vast movement. With the technological boost of television, thousands who had never been part of the community of practice were drawn in. They did not need, nor receive, specific educational or training experiences, but they soon were part of helping to create a nationwide social movement that continues to this day.

In order for flourishing to have similar power, the presence and growth of communities of practice (leading to a social movement engaging a broad swath of society) will be needed. The types of connections cultivated by such a movement will reinforce and extend the spirit of this work into many other arenas beyond business.

An initial budding community of practice into which we invite you is made up of our group of Distinguished Fellows and Fowler Center staff, the Fowler Center's Advisory Board, and those whom we interviewed who asked to be part of our effort. Others we are yet to meet will find us, we hope, through the conversations engendered by the practices and stories in this book.

An allied community of practice is the appreciative inquiry community and that part which is focused on using W-Holistic AI. We expect to see a third group—a corporate community of practice—made up of leading executives who contribute by embedding within their organizations various practices and approaches that we have described and others they have uncovered. We invite them to participate in action research on the impact of those practices and we intend to support them as thinking partners through workshops, conferences, executive education offerings, and performance assessments.

Corporate communities of practice could also naturally develop among companies whose norms and values are aligned with the principles and direction of this work, and for whom there is a sensed readiness to engage. Communities of practice might also develop among companies in a common supply chain. We are committed to creating gatherings for those companies in which all of us can share stories, insights, and practices, tap into cutting-edge research, and be part of new forms of executive education.

As corporate communities of practice develop, on the academic side we expect to see papers, presentations, and collaborations feed the growing AI community. From these we anticipate an abundance of material with which to build constructive "webbing" with other communities beyond the Fowler Center.

Perhaps our greatest value as a community of practice, no matter what the structure, might be this webbing activity, this sharing of experiences and learning with similar groups who have members with a passion for flourishing and sustainability. We see this melded structure with webs to other existing groups evolving into a global community of practice that includes a mix of Sustainable Value, Appreciative Inquiry, Organizational Learning, and related frameworks that promote flourishing.

Over time, these multiple communities of practice should create fertile ground for a much broader movement, with the intent of sweeping vast numbers of people into the stream of this work. While our initial steps might be quite close-in and intentionally planned, our ultimate vision is for this work to develop way beyond our influence.

We realize that the success of everything we have sketched depends in large part on our ability, collectively, with you, to excite, engage, and create value. The more all of us can design for and nurture a sense of "aliveness," the more people will be drawn to this effort. When any one community of practice has served to gather and engage people and their organizations, a piece of the groundwork for a larger movement will have been put in place. All of this work will take time, patience, and persistence. As Marge Piercy writes,

> The people I love the best
> Jump into work head first
>
> . . .
>
> I love people who harness themselves, an ox to a heavy cart,
> who pull like water buffalo, with massive patience
>
> . . .
>
> who do what has to be done, again and again.[2]

We ask ourselves and you: What are the most immediate next steps? What would each of us most like to see happen as a result of this work? What broader role might we and our team play? We look forward to connecting with you and others with whom you may be partnering in a way that gives us all an opportunity to learn more, and to refine and enrich the ideas and practices that relate reflective practices and spirituality to business value, creativity, prosperity, and flourishing.

Our hope is that a global shift in awareness will be engendered through this work, and that increasing numbers of enterprises will seek ways to create sustainable value by fostering an environment in which people can flourish. Our intended result is flourishing companies, and flourishing systems across a broad range of industries, sectors, and geographies.

What we are espousing is not just a mind shift. Yes, we are challenging each of us to make decisions based on broader thinking and possibilities—that kind of mind shift. But there is more to it than that: we believe that for our deepest collective success, as business people and even as a species, the most important shift will be one of heart and spirit. That shift is both challenging and simple; it requires each of us to fully show up, to bring our whole self, our highest self to all of our work, to our conversations and our meetings, to our decision-making. When each of us fully shows up, so too will our sense of interconnectedness and wholeness within, and our sense of connection with others and with the world around us.

An Invitation

In closing, it may be useful for us all to consider what flourishing looks and feels like in our own lives, teams, organizations, and systems. When we recall occasions when we have experienced a flourishing state of connection to ourselves, to others, and to the natural world, we have an opportunity to remember what such a state enabled us to think, feel, and do, and that flourishing is not foreign to us, it is within and around us. We might ask ourselves, if we had access to such a state on a more regular basis, how would it change our orientation to this work? And finally, what possible actions do these ideas suggest as we seek to create flourishing at every scale?

As we gathered recently to celebrate the work that created the book you have in front of you, we began our meeting with the practice of reading a poem, the following one, and reflecting on it. One of us said in the silence that followed the reading, "this Mark Nepo poem is about our work."

The Appointment

What if, on the first sunny day,
on your way to work, a colorful bird
sweeps in front of you down a
street you've never heard of.

You might pause and smile,
a sweet beginning to your day.

Or you might step into that street
and realize there are many ways to work.

You might sense the bird knows something you don't and wander after.

You might hesitate when the bird
turns down an alley. For now
there is a tension: Is what the
bird knows worth being late?

You might go another block or two,
thinking you can have it both ways.
But soon you arrive at the edge
of all your plans.

The bird circles back for you
and you must decide which
appointment you were
born to keep.[3]

Put another way, what changes does the world require of us now, and what different appointments will we keep? Which appointment were you born to keep?

Afterword

David Cooperrider

For the reader who seeks to understand where the future of great business is heading, my advice is: begin with this book. *Flourishing Enterprise* is a complete guide for organizations wishing to bring prosperity and flourishing to the full spectrum of stakeholders that *sustainable value creation* makes possible.

The book, as the reader has experienced by now, is bold, imaginative, and provocative, and it is studded with understandings into what might well become the new North Star for *sustainability* as a field. This is what is so stunning about the book: it's not just about the future, but will actually help shape it—by asking all of us to aspire to something greater than what corporate sustainability typically aims for.

The flourishing enterprise is something every industry leader wants. Flourishing enterprise is about people being inspired every day and bringing their whole selves into the enterprise; it's about innovation arising from everywhere; and it's about realizing remarkable *relationship value* with stakeholders, including customers, communities, and societies, and ultimately with a thriving biosphere. When John Donne said, "No man is an island," he was foreshadowing the major ingredient of flourishing as proposed in this volume: consciousness that everything is connected.

The grammar of interconnection is the business discipline of our age. In the rest of this afterword I build on the achievements of this volume, then amplify a hidden opportunity—a huge one. It relates to a question that I've been studying and that I believe we, as a field, are zeroing in on with an honest answer from which every organization and industry can benefit. That overarching question is this:

How can we most reliably, naturally, and rapidly bring the human side of enterprise to its vital best—to a tangible and irrepressible state of enterprise-wide flourishing inside and outside—and do so in pragmatic ways that break the "sound barriers" to sustainable value creation at a more macro level?

The answer revolves around a profound dynamic called *obliquity*—how, by taking attention away from something, we can actually accomplish even more than if we went directly after it. For example, companies that pursue profit in a straight line, over everything else, very likely will not do as well as those that create a deep emotional connection with a powerful purpose beyond profit. Another example is perhaps even better: When I was invited at the height of the violence to work in South Africa at a center that hosted all the diverse groups coming together to change the country, not one single meeting over the months was on the topic or priority agenda of *ending apartheid*—not one, even though apartheid was in full operation. I was shocked, even confused. Then someone illuminated: "You see, David, you don't get it; apartheid is already done—its dead and done in the minds of millions. Dealing with reducing the negative aspects of apartheid is not our work, it does not and cannot inspire. Every single meeting and minute, as you will see, will be totally focused on new designs for *the post-apartheid* society—we are building a legacy."

And that's what subsequently happened. We all saw it: it was not long, then, when right in front of the world's eyes Mandela and de Klerk spontaneously raised their hands together in a soccer stadium, and that gesture echoed 'round the world. Was apartheid ended? It certainly was. But making it less bad did not change the system. Apartheid was eclipsed. And the massive, systemic process that brought about apartheid's end had been faster and more profound than anyone in the world had predicted. Yes, economic sanctions were part of it, and so was the presence of towering leadership. But there was a genius in the framing. Not one meeting had been about ending apartheid, *yet* that was the result. Obliquity works that way—we don't fall asleep, for example, by putting all our energy into falling asleep. A good night's rest is something that *ensues,* not something one *pursues.* It ensues from something else—perhaps a contented heart, or a good day's work—in fact, the more we pursue it directly, the more restlessness, weariness, and tossing-and-turning we are likely to experience. Many things are that way.

Could it be the same thing with unsustainability? Is doing less harm really the topic?

Where Do We Look to Inspire Large-Scale Change in Sustainable Business?

Though it's never the purpose of a good afterword to retrace a book in its totality, let me try to underscore the essence of this work, while also drawing on ideas and recent discussions by authors in the *Harvard Business Review.* Several of them, including C. K. Prahalad and Ram Nidumolu, share similar concerns: *Where do we look to drive large-scale change for sustainable business?*[1]

We can talk about three levels of change—with Level 3 being the deepest:

Level 1: These changes involve sustainability efforts in *enterprise systems,* strategies, and processes, including stakeholder partnerships, and often result in cost savings and reductions in the harm caused by new products, waste, toxicities, energy systems, and overall footprint. It's here that Design for Environment, life-cycle analysis, and other tools are introduced through training, manuals, videos, and expert analysis.

Level 2: These changes in *organizational culture and identity* are deeper and consist of changes in beliefs, norms, ways of operating, and assumptions about business in society. These assumptions often become sacred company values by which words and deeds become aligned and the sustainability culture of doing less harm becomes embedded, not simply a bolted-on, and at its best becomes so enculturated that it permeates everything—strategy, operations, everyday language, and behavior.

Level 3: These are changes in business leadership's *sense of self* and in leaders' commitment, a shift from trying to do less harm to advancing the sources of positive good—to leave a positive fingerprint or signature on the world. Such change arises from a sense of genuine consciousness of connection, from being inspired internally to be the kind of person we are or want to become, and from belief in the power of positive conscious intention.

As Ram Nidumolu has articulated, the interesting thing is that the change drivers at each level are different, and as the authors of this book have proposed, the third level—call it the spiritual level, the level of deeper meaning and purpose in the interconnected web of life—is most important. It is, as the authors so powerfully detail it, the internal inspiration and personal flourishing that make the difference—being alive with purpose, emotional connection, and full belief in our vast potentials. Consider, for example, any great change agent, from Nelson Mandela to Helen Keller, or extraordinary designers and entrepreneurs, from Janine Benyus, cofounder of the Biomimicry Guild, to the late Ray Anderson, founder of Interface. There are solid reasons why the deeper levels of change have a bigger impact on the shallower levels than vice versa. The change drivers at the first level are return on investment and the business case; change at the second level is catalyzed significantly via external interactions with changing societal expectations; and change at the third level emerges through reflective practices and intrinsic motivation or commitment. If the deeper levels, from the inside outward, have a bigger impact on the shallower levels than the shallower levels have on the deeper levels, then what outcomes might we predict if the third level is weak or absent?

What we would predict is what is happening in far too many organizations. Once the early business gains of sustainability are realized—and to be sure the bottom-line business case today is as exciting and robust as it has ever been—soon enough a ceiling is realized. The nearer companies come to net zero—let's say they are halfway there by cutting fuel costs in half, reducing waste, using less water or precious metals, and so on—the more exhausted the sustainability efforts become. Think of the Sisyphus experience.

Far too many of the first movers in the sustainable business domain have subsequently abandoned sustainability or demoted it from its strategic position to an operational concern. From BP's dislodgment of its original sustainability vision to the uphill battle of Interface's Mount Sustainability, and from Wal-Mart's early "all hands on deck" big splash to Green Mountain Coffee Roasters' growth challenges, there appears a brick wall.

"Climbing Mt. Sustainability gets increasingly harder the closer you get to the peak," said Ray Anderson, "just as climbers of Mt. McKinley show us as they are gasping mightily for air the higher they go."

Goodbye, Good Riddance, Sustainability?

Quite suddenly, in this decade the sustainability advantage has been "discovered" by thousands of companies. The business case—for example, the Tata Group, Google, Herman Miller, Natura, and others highlighted in this volume—as well as studies of "firms of endearment"—that is, firms that are winning the hearts and minds of people, of the customers and communities they serve—is becoming striking.[2] Over the past fifteen years, the stock performance of "Firms of endearment" such as Whole Foods, Starbucks, and others has risen at more than three times the rate of even those remarkable and successful companies highlighted in Jim Collins's research published in *Good to Great*.[3]

Meanwhile, empirical meta-analysis of the human side of enterprise—of employee well-being—has demonstrated that productivity, profits, employee retention, and customer obsession all increase as the level of workplace well-being, particularly employee personal growth, increases.[4] What has not happened, however, is a bringing together of the two domains—the sustainability domain and human flourishing in the workplace—and that's perhaps the most compelling call of this book.

Sustainability initiatives will likely run out of steam, propose the authors, unless we accompany all of the sustainable value tools— life cycle analysis, focus on energy efficiency, net zero goal setting, LEED (Leadership in Energy and Environmental Design) certified buildings, waste-to-wealth efforts, social entrepreneurship, blue ocean strategy, sustainable product design, and more—with a global mind- and spirit-shift in our consciousness of connectedness.

I was in a meeting of CEOs in Brazil and suddenly this point made concrete sense. The debate was over the language of social responsibility. One CEO said that the language of corporate social responsibility—just the language itself, of one entity taking responsibility for the whole—felt like an ethical demand or another external "have to." The CEO was Rodrigo Loures, one of the most successful and respected business leaders in the country, and he said, "It's not about *responsibility for* the whole; it's about *intimacy with* the whole." Read Rodrigo's words once again; they are that important.

What a powerful *quiet recognition*. It changes everything. The shift from responsibility to intimacy does not change the scene as much as it changes perception: we don't wish for our son or daughter or other cherished, close relations to simply survive; we want them to thrive. We want them to flourish, and when they do, we thrill to their success—*because we care;* it's a response that is intrinsic.

Can we expect the same *natural conviction or instinctive response* from our sustainability initiatives? Where can we look for the intrinsic energy and natural motivation to drive large-scale change for sustainable business, whole industries, and sustainable economies? Are there ways to access whole new magnitudes of change capacity?

The authors of this volume say the answer is yes, but we need new language, reframing, and a new and deeper starting place. And I love their first move. Are they really saying "goodbye, good riddance, sustainability"? This is not a trivial change. Not that long ago the word *sustainability* was unknown. Today the field is flooded with headlines about producing sustainable brands that reduce waste, creating carbon offsets, designing more energy-efficient facilities, aiming toward zero landfill, associating their marketing with green advertising, turning bottom-of-the-pyramid populations into new markets, and now, for some of the most courageous, becoming transparent about the true market costs of externalities. Sustainability noise is everywhere.

The word *sustainability* is troublesome for two reasons. The first is that *words matter.* As Wittgenstein once said, "the limits of language are the limits of our worlds"—and in other writings, colleagues and I have traced how *words enable worlds.*[5] Think of how fast Malcolm Gladwell's language of the "tipping point" has spread, and how attractive the concept became to inspired social media pioneers and CEOs such as Jeff Bezos, founder of Amazon.com. What if Gladwell had instead called it "sensitive dependence on initial conditions" like systems scientists do? Or think about the field of psychology, obsessed for more than a century with "mental illness," and how stagnant and stale the field became, until the 1990s, when Marty Seligman called for the study of *thriving*, a search for the elements of the "good life," and the positive psychology of "human strengths."[6]

An amazing sea change happened almost overnight as we turned attention to "learned optimism" and "emotional intelligence" and nutritional excellence for "superimmunity"—not just health as the absence of disease. In the field of organization development we used to be obsessed with the topic of "low morale" in companies (remember the low-morale surveys). Then a bit later the bar was raised to the study of normal "job satisfaction." But why weren't we studying the positively deviant dynamics of thriving and excellence and the most exceptional high-engagement systems?

Well, today we are, and lessons from positive organizational scholarship and appreciative inquiry studies into what gives life to human systems when they are most alive have shown something curious: *human systems grow in the direction of what we most persistently and deeply ask questions about, the topics we study,* precisely because those topic choices put a frame around what we discover, feed what we soon talk about, and become the resources for what we design. And it's true, when you really think about it. All the studies in the world about the causes of "low morale" will not teach us one thing about the dynamics and sources of inspired workplaces where people bring their hearts and souls every day, just as if they were the owners of the business. Earlier I related my huge surprise at how in South Africa every meeting way before the end of apartheid was not framed in terms of ending apartheid or reducing its harms—instead, every single gathering was united in a larger aim: the design of the post-apartheid system. What if we in turn assume that *unsustainability* is already achieved—that it is dead and gone as a respected or valued practice? Then we need to ask, what's next? Could we achieve the reversal of the harms of unsustainability faster, in obliquity terms, by focusing on something else altogether?

This is exactly what the authors of this book have achieved with their focus on flourishing. The word *sustainability* no longer inspires—and perhaps never did—as long as it's framed largely as surviving instead of thriving, as "doing less bad" instead of achieving a world of flourishing. Think about a gym shoe company that asks its designers to design a gym shoe that does less harm—for example, that biodegrades in a few decades as opposed to a hundred years. Is *that* inspiring? Not really. Now imagine a gym shoe company that aims at blue ocean opportunity and positive regeneration of ecosystems. So they ask their designers, "Can you design us a gym shoe that's made from biodegradable materials, appeals to young people, generates a viral social media buzz so there are no advertising costs, and is produced in net positive solar energy facilities—and by the way, when the shoes are done you simply plant them in your backyard and they turn into a tree or flower?" Indeed, this is not hypothetical at all. It's happening, and the fashionable Netherlands-based company that's doing it is called OAT. This is not sustainability as surviving. It's about designing economies that bloom and flourish—as an intentional design process. To be sure, similar breakthroughs can be seen in great designs such as Bill McDonough's architectural designs for flourishing and designer Bruce Mau's massive change exhibitions. So does this mean goodbye, good riddance, *sustainability?*

The way I read it is no. What the authors are speaking about, however, is a crucial, much-needed reconceptualization. Imagine if every time we heard the word *sustainability* we saw in banner lights "sustainability as flourishing" rather than "sustainability as surviving." In business vocabulary that's what the authors call sustainable *value* creation—value that leads to or enhances the potentials for flourishing and prosperity across the full spectrum of stakeholder relationships, and value that simultaneously leads to or elevates the potential for flourishing and prosperity for the business. Full-spectrum flourishing is a sustainability+ movement, one that invites fresh explorations, opens exciting new vistas, and unites fertile dialogues across diverse disciplines from biomimicry to business strategy, and from advanced technology and neuroscience to spirituality.

This is a big achievement. Just as sustainability has hit the peak of the S curve, where soon there will be a predictable decline, this book provides the call and the connective synapses where new and high-potential interdisciplinary sparks can be ignited.

Re-centering on the Human Spirit

What I admire most about this volume is its courage to take up the "spiritual adventure" behind sustainability-as-flourishing, the search for meaning, purpose, and value that becomes an end in itself. One of the truths of our time is this hunger, deep in people all across the economy, for realizing that their lives count, and count affirmatively, that they are a positive force for the future we envision. Is it an accident that young people are flocking to a company such as Google, which provides dedicated programs for personal development, wellness, and nutritional excellence; hiking trails and solar-inspired buildings; meditation courses; and collaborative teaming—as well as daring, world-changing projects such as the one aimed at bringing Internet information, and connectivity to bear on eradicating extreme poverty within a generation?

When you visit the Googleplex (the headquarters of Google in Mountain View, California), as I did just last week, you see extraordinary investment in human excellence. Do you know what's perhaps the most popular course by demand at Google? It's the one offered by Chade-Meng Tan, employee number 107, and it's based on his book *Search Inside Yourself: The Unexpected Path to Achieving Success, Happiness (and World Peace).*[7] Talk about success *by* design: while most companies espouse that people are the most important element, at the Googleplex one could sense genuine commitment being acted on in every nook and cranny of the campus. In one meeting, I watched a team that was on fire exploring the implications of a world where sensors, via "the internet of things," will be able to cut world energy costs in half, where ocean temperature fluctuations can be monitored just as a mother closely attunes to her newborn's fever, and where global vital signs of species, toxicities, and subtle climate changes can be sensitively examined 24/7 everywhere. One person shared what it's like to work on a world-changing legacy project. "We are" she said, "waking up to our earth's vital signs."

All of this is consistent with the hypothesis explored in this book—that organizations that build on the human factor to foster flourishing in terms of *inner development* will be more successful as sustainability+*flourishing enterprises,* which ultimately will drive sustainable value creation for the business and for a better, more *flourishing world* (see Figure A.1). There is, as the authors propose, a critical trajectory here, and it begs a whole series of important questions: What will happen to sustainability efforts in the absence of a flourishing workplace? What do we mean by flourishing, versus languishing, in personal human terms? Can we really influence the character of human beings (for example, create in them concern for humanity, empathy, wisdom, social intelligence, creativity, ethical affirmation of life, mindfulness, generativity and concern for future generations, and so on)? And then we might ask: Can the trajectory work bidirectionally instead of only unidirectionally? What if we reversed this sensible arrangement? Might we achieve the prize of a flourishing workplace—inspired, innovative, engaged, caring, aware, and generative—by starting with the third stage in Figure A.1 and then moving from left to right? Could it be that the creation of more flourishing societies and ecosystems inspires more flourishing organizations and stakeholder collaborations, which in turn creates fertile conditions in which people may flourish—thus traversing the proposition in reverse?

We know from systems theory that when any two events are interdependent, identifying one as cause and the other as effect is an arbitrary designation. Both Peter Senge [8] and Karl Weick[9] have shown that in causal loops no variable is any more or less important than any other variable. In a loop you can, at least theoretically, start the sequence anywhere you want by changing any event or variable.

In the rest of this afterword, I add an additional dimension for leaders to consider in terms of an action agenda or positive pathway. For me the implications of looking at the authors' proposition in reverse order are not only interesting but also powerfully actionable as leverage points for one remarkable source of business value that will never run out. It has to do with self-amplifying loops and virtuous circles. "Managers get in trouble," argues Weick, "because they forget to think in circles."[10]

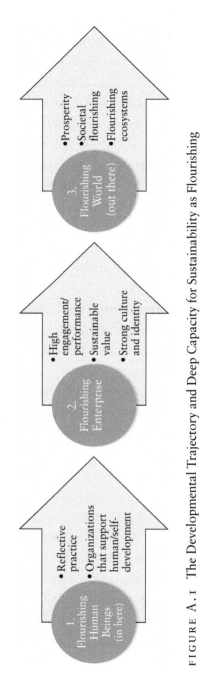

FIGURE A.1   The Developmental Trajectory and Deep Capacity for Sustainability as Flourishing

There Can Be No Flourishing "In Here"
Without Flourishing "Out There"

One of the high-point moments in my recent memory is a series of almost a dozen lectures I did in duet fashion with Marty Seligman across Australia. Hosted by the professional services firm Pricewater-houseCoopers, we spoke to hundreds of executives in the financial, health care, manufacturing, education, and information technology fields. Marty is well-known around the world as the father of the "positive psychology" movement, which is all about the scientific study of the good life—what it is, where it is happening, and what nurtures it—including the strengths and systems that enable individuals and communities to thrive. The field is founded on the belief that people want to lead meaningful and fulfilling lives, to cultivate what is best within themselves and others, and to enhance their experiences of love, work, and play. In its early stages, positive psychology set forward three central pillars of concern: the study of positive emotions, the identification of positive individual traits or strengths, and the discovery and design of positive institutions.[11] Understanding positive emotions entails the study of contentment with the past, flourishing in the present, and hope and optimism for the future.[12] Understanding positive individual traits consists of the cataloguing and study of our highest human strengths and virtues, such as the capacity for love, courage, ethical compassion, resilience, creativity, curiosity, integrity, self-knowledge, justice, spirituality, and wisdom.[13] Understanding positive institutions, as my colleagues and I have defined them, entails the study of how organizations and communities themselves can become vehicles for the elevation, magnification, and refraction of our highest human strengths *beyond the organization* and out into the world.[14]

In our talks, Seligman shared a preliminary outline of what would become his next major book, *Flourish: A Visionary New Understanding of Well-Being,*[15] and I shared the theory of how we become what we study, that is, how our appreciative inquiries into the true, the

better, and the possible actually create a momentum and new language of life for scientific construction of social reality.

We explored the many dimensions of flourishing, and Marty
shared the well-researched dimensions of the good life—the five pillars of the flourishing life—through the acronym PERMA. In many
respects the PERMA model is a great summation of the extraordinary
findings of positive psychology from the past decade. *P* stands for
the study of positive emotion and explores questions such as "what
good are positive emotions such as hope, inspiration, and joy?" *E*
signifies "the engaged life," or a life in which our unique strengths
are engaged, and how this pillar of well-being and growth is actively
applied to the workplace. *R* underscores high-quality relationships
and the centrality of the Other in a theory of flourishing. *M* is all
about the role of meaning—about how, without a life of meaning
and purpose, there can be no deep sense of flourishing. Finally, *A,*
for accomplishment, is about the part of human happiness or well-
being that is not fleeting but enduring.

Following the introduction of PERMA, it was my opportunity
to explore not just the individual psychology but also the opportunity for institutions. My call was to share observations on the most
flourishing workplaces I had seen over some thirty years in the field
of management. What surprised even me was this: *every single one
of the most extraordinary examples I spotlighted were organizations
leading the way in the sustainable value domain.* In shared real-life
video clips—scenes from our large-group Appreciative Inquiry Summits
with systems such as Fairmount Minerals, which soon came to be an
industry-leading star financially and was awarded the top corporate
citizen award by the U.S. Chamber of Commerce; scenes from our
work with Kofi Annan and five hundred CEOs to design the strategies
for the UN Global Compact; scenes from our whole-system-in-the-
room Appreciative Inquiry summits with cities such as Cleveland with
their "a green city on a blue lake" work; and our strategic planning
summits with whole states, such as our work with Massachusetts gov-

ernor Deval Patrick to convene the state's partnership with National Grid, a network of more than three hundred energy organizations working to design the pathway to renewable energy transformation. In each case, what we observed and tracked was a remarkable rise in each of the dimensions of PERMA's flourishing. So what exactly was happening here? As people worked together on new designs for "out there"—for example, the restoration of a waterway to its purest potentials—there was, in palpable terms, a PERMA response, and the thought crossed my mind, What do we know about the enhancement of human capacities through the power of restoring and revitalizing nature? Can companies, by engaging people in radically reducing energy watts, also in a reverse fashion actually produce more human energy?

After a couple of such talks, I realized that it was not a minor discovery or finding. For over thirty years I have been active in the applied side of organization change theory, helping to guide strategic planning and major organization development initiatives in organizations such as National Grid, Apple, Sherwin Williams, Clarke, VitaMix, GOJO Industries, and companies participating in the UN Global Compact, including Novo Nordisk, Telefónica, and Tata Industries.[16] Obviously, over my decades in the field of management, I have seen a myriad of developments: the birth of the World Wide Web, the re-engineering of the corporation, participative management, the quality revolution, and many more. Because of my organizational science background, I've also had a keen interest in how each particular management innovation has affected the human side of enterprise—things like inspiration and hope, engagement, entrepreneurship and innovation, and collaborative capacity. And herein lies my number one observation, after thirty years in the real world: *there is nothing that brings out the best in human enterprise faster, more consistently, or more powerfully than calling the whole organization to design innovations to meet humanity's greatest challenges.*

As soon as people come together to accomplish "doing good" out there—by concentrating and connecting their strengths in the service of building a better organization, or city, or world—they begin to activate the PERMA mechanisms *for their own and others' flourishing.*

Put another way, the active pursuit of sustainable value creation is not only about serving or satisfying external stakeholders; it is also core to individual flourishing inside the firm. Sustainable value creation and shared well-being reinforce one another and thereby serve to launch a far-reaching exploration: What is the link between advancing sustainability for a flourishing earth and the flourishing of the human side of enterprise? Precisely how might an organization's quest for sustainable value not only bring out the best on the outside—helping to advance a better society or world—but also almost simultaneously bring out the best on the "inside"—in the flourishing of people, the quality of their relationships, their health, their performance, and their capacity for growth, resilience, and positive change?

To be sure, this is not simply a theoretical question. If the results are as I am suggesting, then this is big news for the human resources industry and for every single leader who would love to have a workplace that is alive with purpose, meaning, passion, high engagement, trust, inspired innovation, and collaborative agility. Could it be that the quest for sustainable value—when everyone in the corporation is galvanized for strategic sustainable innovation in the service of a more flourishing world—is *the most significant human development opportunity of the twenty-first century?*

A well-known quote attributed to Aristotle begins to explain why: "We do not act rightly because we have virtue or excellence, but we rather have those because we have acted rightly. We are what we repeatedly do. Excellence, then, is not an act but a habit."

The Power of Mirror Flourishing

Elsewhere I have speculated further with my colleague Ron Fry on this sustainable value, or S-PERMA, link. We've called it the *mirror flourishing effect.*[17] We could have labeled it many other things, and we considered them all—reverse flourishing, positive transference, the so-called helpers high, reflexive flourishing, or the hypothesis on "why good things happen to good people." (See Stephen Post's comprehensive review of the latter hypothesis.[18])

But the word *mirror* seemed to offer the conceptual richness we were looking for. In recent neuroscience, for example, in exploring the relationship between connections and contagion, there has been the conceptualization of a biological basis for empathy, the spread of emotion, and interaction consonance, which is the property of being alike, in harmony with, becoming at one with, or *growing* together. It's called the *mirror neuron system*, in which parts of the brain light up when we merely observe a tennis match—just *as if* we ourselves were actually playing the match.[19]

The discovery of the mirror neuron is shaking up numerous scientific disciplines and shifting the understanding of culture, empathy, philosophy, language, imitation, and the spread of happiness across networks in a synchronized or consonant way. The concept of the mirror neuron helps explain the dynamic of consonance across living systems. Of course this growing together can work for both good and ill. When our companies are involved in destroying nature or value in the world—think, for example, of how the people of BP were and still are feeling in relation to the horrifying images and experience of the 2010 Gulf oil spill—it's easy to sense how the human side of that enterprise might understandably enter a state of dissonant discontent or languishing, the very opposite of flourishing. There are colossal human costs to being part of destroying value, and much of the heartsickness you see in our world today happens because we know, deep down, that environmental and economic collapse are not separate from our lives.

Mirror flourishing suggests an intimacy of relations between entities to the point where we can posit that there is no outside and inside, only the creative unfolding of an entire *field of relations* or connections. As Martin Buber once wrote, "In the beginning is the relationship."[20] In a similar manner, the metaphor of the mirror neuron also helps us erase the traditional boundaries of separation.

*I define mirror flourishing as the concrescence, flourishing, or grow-
ing together that happens naturally and reciprocally when we actively
engage in or witness the acts that help nature flourish, others flourish,
or the world as a whole to flourish.*

When I spoke to the OAT entrepreneurs who created a business for
"shoes that bloom," you could sense a joy and delight in their words
that were contagious. I too smiled when I wore my first pair of those
sneakers. And then the emotion spread: it was repeated all over again
when my children opened their presents, and then again when they
asked if I could get the shoes as gifts for their friends. Does flourishing
via the conveying power of *sustainably significant action* flow through
networks, just as a virus might? Perhaps. In fact, the sociology of networks shows that when a friend living less than a mile away becomes
happy, it can increase the probability that you are happy by 25 percent
or more—in other words, our emotions and states of well-being, even
dimensions of our physical health, flow quietly through our connections. Social and ecological networks, including those with the more-
than-human world, are sensitive, intricate, and perhaps even hardwired.

Mirror flourishing is more that a tangential episode; it is a predictable and observable trajectory. It is, in a word, a developmental force
if we know how to harness it: we can intentionally and consciously
create a flourishing workplace by extending beyond ourselves, by
working to build a better world that flourishes. We gain life inside
by nurturing life outside. And this, as we shall see, is a testable hypothesis: people who experience themselves, their organizations, and
their relations as successfully and innovatively working to build a
more sustainable-flourishing future will experience higher levels of
well-being as expressed by the many dimensions of PERMA.

The implications of this hypothesis are of course enormous. The
phrase *do good, do well* becomes more than a social responsibility
mantra. Of all the things that bring out the best in human beings,
one of the principle ones is the mirroring effect that happens when
we help bring out the best in nature and others. The reality of mirror

flourishing, when it is experienced most authentically, might well be *the human development business opportunity of our time,* at least under conditions such as those found in whole-system change practice, like the Appreciative Inquiry Sustainable Design Factory, or what Ilma Barros and Chris Laszlo have termed W-Holistic-AI.

What we are seeing emerge in our observations is an incomparable way to engage and energize the entire workforce—a way in which people come alive with purpose, meaning, hope, inspiration, and intrinsically motivated accomplishment. Mirror flourishing speaks to the unified and integral two-way flow between business and the world— this fundamental blurring of the boundaries of "in here" and "out there"—and to the possibility that when we help life "out there" to flourish, we cannot help but benefit ourselves as well. I'll never forget when, in a five-hundred-person sustainable design summit at Fairmount Minerals, an employee team came up with a new business idea for a $15 sand water filter.[21] Ultimately it would be deployed in forty-four countries, saving lives all over the world. But it would also benefit the business; the market distribution was not so much charity as a win-win sustainable value proposition. The cross-functional team was on fire and inspired, filled with pride in the company. And like a resonant bell, this work "out there" reverberated all the way down the line of sight into many aspects of the everyday work experience. Can you imagine people lining up in droves to work for a sand-mining company? We're not talking Silicon Valley glitz and glamor. We're talking about sand loader operators, engineers, finance specialists, and production supervisors. That's what happened to this award-winning enterprise.

Outside the sustainability literature, even without a name for it, there are now more than five hundred scientific studies on this doing good–doing well dynamic. Stephen Post has summarized many of them in his book *Why Good Things Happen to Good People.* He argues that this doing good–doing well dynamic is "the most potent force on the planet."[22] If you engage in helping activities as a teen, for example, you will still be reaping health benefits sixty or seventy years later. But in all of this research there is not one study related to sustainability work, to what happens to us when we restore nature, or the human impact in corporations that are leading the world in sustainable value. Obviously the possibilities are wide open and vast, just as the current volume suggests.

The reversal of so much of active disengagement in the workplace, as well as of depression and heartsickness in our culture at large, might well be easier to accomplish than we think. Imagine the positive-mirror flourishing effect of millions of sustainable value initiatives reverberating, scaling up, and amplifying. Imagine sustainability-as-flourishing and the predictable dynamic of mirror flourishing being actively harnessed as a massive human development leverage point. This is obliquity in action. It's worth repeating. "We *are* what we repeatedly do," said Aristotle. "Excellence, then, is not an act but a habit."

When you read this book for the second or third stint, take some time for reflection. What you will hear is the message that each one of us is a seed, a quiet promise, and that through *our* reflective practices, business has the opportunity to be one of the most creative forces on the planet. And you will find that you are not alone. Many people today, like you, share the hope that the twenty-first century can become, without one moment of delay, an unprecedented era of innovation in which businesses can excel, people can thrive, and nature can flourish. This amazing volume, *Flourishing Enterprise,* calls us to exciting new definitions, new practices, and a new mind. It invites us to aim higher and deeper at the same time. And it charts a reflective pathway for a reunion of prosperity with full-spectrum flourishing. Is it possible to sum it up in a nutshell? The authors say yes, and here's how: *"by working reflectively smarter, collectively smarter, and spiritually smarter."*[23]

David Cooperrider
Fairmount Minerals Professor of Social Entrepreneurship
Weatherhead School of Management
Case Western Reserve University

The Odyssey of This Book

We began with a bold question: Might spirituality, broadly understood, be an essential ingredient in helping businesses to thrive in
service of a flourishing world? This query launched the multiyear
exploration at the intersection of sustainability and spirituality that
has resulted in the book you have in your hands. Looking for answers, nine of us at the Fowler Center for Sustainable Value came
together around this focal question. Composed of six Distinguished
Fellows and three Fowler Center colleagues, our team sensed that the
unusual and important territory we were exploring might summon
yet unknown talents and energies—offering the equivalent of building a ship in the way that Saint-Exupéry suggests:

> If you want to build a ship,
> don't drum up people to collect wood
> and
> don't assign them tasks and work
> but rather teach them
> to long for
> the endless immensity of the sea.[1]

Seeking to be shipbuilders for our time, we began to search for
ways to engage people in experiences that foster the equivalent of
"longing for the endless immensity of the sea," that is, longing for,
dreaming of, a world in which businesses contribute profitably to creating a path on which all of life can flourish on the earth forever. We
wondered, do such enterprises already exist? How are they led and
managed? What results do they produce and how scalable are they?

The concept of *flourishing,* with its sense of vitality, was the first anchor of our work, and it proved to be a powerful draw for executives who were eager to go beyond existing notions of sustainability.[2] Flourishing is so compelling, they said, because it more clearly embodies the goal of sustainability. *Spirituality,* our second anchor, was equally powerful but more polarizing. It resonated immediately with one slice of the business community. Yet it was loaded with associations that for others did not seem to belong in the workplace. For many of the business people we engaged in our inquiry, the term presented a challenge. We needed better ways to think and talk about the territory.

More than a few eyebrows shot up when we mentioned the mission on which we were embarking. Nevertheless, we were encouraged to set sail, spurred on by business people from every walk of life— every culture, sector, demographic, and industry affiliation—who told us they thirsted for more meaningful conversations about the topic. As one senior executive put it, "Being centered in knowing oneself, through inner transformation and spirituality, and knowing one's life work creates a new conversation about what it means to do good in this world. It will ultimately shape a new business culture where the environmental, social, and economic dimensions taken together can create value. . . . Gaining competitive advantage in the future is going to take [such] a whole-person approach."[3]

A New Leadership Orientation

Spirituality was hardly a mainstream business topic when we began this work in 2011, even though there were encouraging signs that it was taking hold in companies as diverse as Google, Green Mountain Coffee Roasters, and Kyocera. Most often, matters of spirit remained a side conversation, a topic whispered and touched on only obliquely. Some corporate leaders were choosing neutral or "business-friendly" language to point to spirituality. David Baker, a manager at Boeing Commercial Airplanes, expressed it this way: "We link spirituality to value creation—the purpose of an organization is to create value—

which is also about stewardship." He observed the growing popularity of organizational change methods such as Appreciative Inquiry and Theory U, which companies such as Boeing are using to begin collective reflection about values. He pointed to the relational dimension of these efforts, the need to build trusting connections: "For people to open their hearts—you have to create trust—and it is a very spiritual thing. Here (at Boeing) the spirituality language has to be more businesslike, such as trust. . . . " Doing so produced startling results: it gave employees and stakeholders a newfound reservoir of energy and creativity, driving them as few other corporate initiatives did to solve complex business problems and engage collaboratively across departments and supply chains.

We were also hearing prominent business leaders speak publicly about spirituality. Many of them placed it in the pragmatic context of what it takes to succeed in business. Executive chairman Bill Ford, in an hour-long interview as part of the 2013 Wisdom 2.0 conference,[4] was frank about the role that reflective practice, particularly his long-time regular mindfulness meditation, played in his ability to lead the Ford Motor Company and to navigate some very difficult times in the organization. In talking about the difficulty of staying true to his understanding of environmental challenges when those understandings were considered "foolish, stupid, or worse" by some, he said, "I believed that if I stuck the course I could really help change the trajectory of our business and all of industry. . . . What I didn't realize is how long it would take. I did believe always that it was the right path." Ford noted the calmness he found in his meditation practice and credited it with allowing him to stay focused yet compassionate through the recent economic downturn, in which two competitors went bankrupt while Ford managed to weather the storm.

John Mackey, cofounder of Whole Foods and author of *Conscious Capitalism*, has widely expressed his views that business leaders need to possess "higher emotional and spiritual intelligence" and should demonstrate a commitment to helping their employees feel "self-actualized." He argues that this orientation is fundamentally about creating value and finding new ways to help everyone win.[5]

Google offers its employees in-house classes with such titles as "The Neuroscience of Empathy" and "Search Inside Yourself."[6] Similar practices and programs have emerged at Sun Life Financial, General Mills, eBay, Medtronic, Twitter, Facebook, Kaiser Permanente, and Plantronics. The voices of other business leaders who are emphasizing spirituality and linking it to sustainability include Jochen Zeitz at Puma, Chip Conley of Joie De Vivre Hospitality, K. V. Kamath at Infosys, and Marcelo Cardoso at Natura.

When we began our investigation, these organizations were creating and innovating cooperatively across silos, both within their business units and with external partners and stakeholders. They were regularly accessing the deepest source of their employees' collective creativity, drawing on intuition and entrepreneurial spirit to reach levels of peak performance far above their industry averages.

The Challenge of Creating Business and World Benefit

Still, spirituality seemed to hover at the fringe of the business world, part of a more personal side to our places of work. For some business people, those most wary of our exploration, the very word *spirituality* became a showstopper: they could not seem to get past the *S* word once it was brought up. Perhaps they held to the view that faith is a private matter, or that our exploration violated the right to be atheist. Or perhaps they found the word *spirituality* too "celestial," too ethereal, as if it came from a never-never land and simply does not belong in the hard-nosed world of business.

We considered ditching the term. Yet it remained our own sense, and the sense of many of the executives to whom we spoke, that spirituality (as distinct from religion) was at the heart of effective management in complex business environments in which sustainability pressures and opportunities were becoming key success factors. If we

wanted to strengthen the movement from sustainability to flourishing, we had to take the spiritual dimension head-on.

So, throughout this book we chose not to mince our words. It
would have been easier to speak only about reflective practices that
create a sense of wellness, leading ultimately to the necessary conditions for flourishing. Yet the arena in which these dimensions converge is spirituality. In the final analysis, we would have done no
one a service by ducking the issue. In addition to *spirituality*, terms
such as *connectedness* and *wholeness* are also woven throughout our
work. Finding language that is inclusive of a wide range of viewpoints
and practices while remaining relevant to the work of management
posed a huge challenge. Our solution was to use a range of terms
and concepts to emphasize shared perspectives and ideas, rather than
to choose one term or phrase doggedly over another. The idea that
there are reinforcing relationships among spirituality, a sense of connectedness, caring, and flourishing may be hard to understand (which
only means that too little has been said about it), at least initially.
Yet those reinforcing relationships are becoming critical to the tasks
of leadership and management.

Our motives for this endeavor were pragmatic rather than esoteric.
We were interested in figuring out through our studies what enables
enterprises to excel and people to thrive in service of a flourishing
world. We wanted to learn how this happens so that we (and others)
could make more of it happen.

We wondered, what was driving early movers? Customers and
employees in every business sector increasingly expect an organization to have a positive impact on society and on the natural environment, with no trade-off in its financial or operational performance.
Radical transparency and declining natural resources are opening
new business opportunities for enterprises with the right mindset
and the know-how to take advantage of those opportunities. People
everywhere are hungering for meaning in their work and for work
in service of a better world.[7]

We realized that although these dynamics may appear new, the forces moving us in this direction have been building over time. As has been the case for so many management ideas at the leading edge, it was Peter Drucker who anticipated the growing importance that spirituality would play at work. In his 1959 book *Landmarks of Tomorrow,* he wrote, "Society needs a return to spiritual values—not to offset the material but to make it fully productive."[8] Drucker's insight became a cornerstone in thinking of the flourishing enterprise: just as sustainability is no longer about having to choose between doing good and doing well, spirituality is not an aspect of life that we need instead of material success, but rather a guide to its place in our lives.

We could see that corporate executives sometimes stumble on this reality. Janice Marturano stands out as a case in point. After years of managing complex litigation and acquisition projects as a senior executive and Deputy General Counsel at General Mills, she felt completely burned out. Following a leadership retreat led by mindfulness expert Jon Kabat-Zinn, she began to replenish her strength and to cultivate a self-awareness that eventually led to her professional renewal. She reflected that mindfulness practices helped her to "clearly and more consistently observe that we're connected in a million ways to everything around us." She continued, "We're connected to people, to community, to nature." As she went deeper into this practice, the benefits she experienced included greater focus, an ability to be less judgmental, heightened physical awareness, the capacity to "see things anew," and more patience in working with others.[9] Janice added, "It's about training our minds to be more focused, to see with clarity, to have spaciousness for creativity and to feel connected." Among senior executives who have followed her lead and learned mindfulness meditation, 80 percent have reported improvement in the quality of their decisions, and 89 percent have said they became better listeners.[10] Is it religious? One executive's answer: "There is no religion associated with bringing attention to the breath. Anyone can learn this."

The Quest for Connectedness

What shared beliefs launched this collective quest? First, we believed we needed to uncover a stronger pull—a more compelling motivation—for pursuing flourishing than what was experienced in most business sustainability efforts. We could see that sustainability strategies, when driven primarily by the quest for competitive advantage, were failing to produce desired macro-level outcomes, whether related to business prosperity, healthier individuals, or dynamically stable global systems. In every sector, companies making only the business case for sustainability were falling short in providing both the financial returns expected by investors and the solutions to global challenges demanded by stakeholders.[11] While hopes were high and champions were working hard, we had to admit that results were disappointing overall.

Second, we believed that successful business efforts to make sustainability central to the enterprise in a meaningful way depend on long-term vision. That vision needs to function as an arc that goes beyond the CEO's three- to five-year horizon. It needs to be longer than even the strategist's seven-year plan or even the policymaker's fifteen- to fifty-year window. It requires the kind of vision that it once took to build cathedrals: a line of sight to a 150-year "attractor," from which all the important business designs, decisions, and actions could spring. With that line of sight comes the understanding that others will follow in our path and continue the work that reflects a commitment to flourishing enterprise.

Third, we believed that a sense of connection—to our own life purpose, to others, and to the natural world—is essential to flourishing and to unlocking our full potential both individually and collectively. Yet we humans function as if we've lost awareness of our connectedness or as if it has severely diminished over time. We sought to understand how that persistent diminishment has contributed to the difficulty that business people now face in consistently taking actions that support prosperity and flourishing. We began to explore and collect individual, organizational, and system-wide practices that could help restore this core sensibility.

Our hypothesis pointed us to the quality of connectedness—to self, to purpose, to others, and to the natural world. We began to see that the world in which businesses must thrive is increasingly complex and interconnected, and it is a world in which embedded sustainability has become a "need to have" rather than a "nice to have." We could see that factors other than spirituality, such as physical health, emotional well-being, and work-life balance, were also important in producing individual flourishing. But we kept returning to the sense of connectedness based on spiritual experience and fostered by reflective practice that can enable individuals to engage in qualitatively more powerful ways of thinking and acting.

We were especially interested in spiritual awareness that leads both to a greater sense of connectedness *and* to greater involvement with global sustainability challenges. Many people today are awakening to different spiritual practices, some of which, such as yoga and mindfulness meditation, are becoming increasingly mainstream. But these can afford an escape from, rather than a pathway into, deeper engagement in the very real problems of society. Monastic Christians and Hindu sadhus may contribute to the world around them through their subtle vibrations,[12] but most spiritual traditions also have a strong ethic of service to others as the necessary complement to personal cultivation.

Our work together led us to see that it is only through the new beliefs and experiences fostered by repeated reflective practices that we can build the necessary foundations for caring that enable businesses to be sustainable in any meaningful sense of the word. We have come to believe that when we are individually and collectively conscious of our place as a node in a vast and interconnected world, when we are able to experience feelings of purpose and harmony with all that is, we are able to undertake intentional actions that habitually incorporate caring for others and for future generations—and actions taken from that awareness are now vital to success at every scale, including the vitality of the planet.

There is an ancient story, "The Jewel Net of Indra," that touches on this notion of profound connectedness at all levels of the world around us:

Far away in the heavenly abode of the great god Indra, there is a wonderful net which has been hung by some cunning artificer in such a manner that it stretches out infinitely in all directions. In accordance with the extravagant tastes of deities, the artificer has hung a single glittering jewel in each "eye" of the net, and since the net itself is infinite in dimension, the jewels are infinite in number. There hang the jewels, glittering like stars in the first magnitude, a wonderful sight to behold. If we now arbitrarily select one of these jewels for inspection and look closely at it, we will discover that in its polished surface there are reflected all the other jewels in the net, infinite in number. Not only that, but each of the jewels reflected in this one jewel is also reflecting all the other jewels, so that there is an infinite reflecting process occurring.[13]

It is this image of an interconnected world that lies at the heart of the flourishing enterprise.

The Story of How We Wrote the Book

Writing a book with eight other authors has many challenges and many rewards. First, when you mention that you are writing a book with eight other authors, you are likely to be met with raised eyebrows. "You're each writing your own individual chapters, I presume," is often the comeback. When this assumption has been made, we have smiled back and said, "No, nine of us are writing one book, together."

Second, such a collaborative effort can be a daunting task even in the simplest circumstances. Differences in geography and busy schedules allowed for only four face-to-face, one-day meetings of all the authors, augmented by the exchange of many phone calls and e-mails over the three years of conceptualization and writing.

Third, most of us did not know one another before we joined this project. Can you imagine nine strong-minded leaders from a range of sustainability-related professions and vastly different backgrounds, with more than three hundred collective years of individual success, coming to alignment enough on multiple concerns while just getting to know one another?

Across these many challenges, our attention remained fixed on the important contribution our work could offer. We lived with a strong sense of shared purpose, a collective willingness to join and partner, and the sense of high stakes that had been simmering in each of us individually for many years. We were not of one mind, but we continued to choose to come together, to find a way to serve a higher purpose, a way that not one of us was capable of finding on her or his own.

We had been invited by the board of the Fowler Center to explore what it meant to "connect the dots" between the domains of sustainability and spirituality. When we came together the first time, we were well aware that this was relatively new territory and could be sensitive terrain for each of us, and for our readers. We began our task by conducting a broad and deep review of the scholarly literature, talking with each other via regular conference calls, and conducting our own primary research, which included interviewing scores of business leaders, practitioners, and scholars. Most of those we interviewed encouraged us to pursue our goal and share our findings broadly. This became an inspirational nudge that helped motivate us to achieve our collective vision for this work. We didn't know where this path would ultimately take us. We honed our premise, explored various framings, struggled over key definitions, and debated which representative reflective practices to include. We had been invited into this assignment not just because of our common interests, but also for the ways in which we are different.

Once we agreed on the book's basic structure, we split into subgroups, each of us devoting ourselves to the parts of the book to which we felt we could best contribute. We all wrote. Chris Laszlo took the lead in organizing the book, and he and Judy Brown wove together everyone's written contributions. Our individual expertise, which is normally a great gift, was often a challenge as we worked within this collaborative structure. Listening was key. It encouraged the sharing of perspectives. We knew this would not have been the same book with the voice of any one of us missing.

We faced the need to stretch ourselves and bring out the best from each other. One or another of us may have momentarily lost the ability to speak, or to listen, or to honor another's words, or to grow comfortable with our philosophical differences. Thankfully we had our reflective practices: the very ones we have outlined in our book, in fact. We often used them during meetings. We found them an invaluable resource whenever one or another of us felt lost about our work. Again and again we returned to the passionate purpose that none of us wanted to set aside: the 150-year project of humans and all other species flourishing on the earth forever. The rewards we experienced from this process came from our accelerated learning, the experience of connection we felt with one another, and ultimately the inner nourishment we experienced as our mutual caring grew.

The challenges, differences, and choices faced by our group can be viewed as parallel to the interconnected challenges that human-kind faces. Solutions will depend on new thinking and will require diverse groups to come together. The members of these groups will be distinct in their ways of thinking, in their ways of doing, and in their ways of being, but they will have to come together in order to design a successful path to a flourishing world. In many ways our group of authors manifested surges and lapses not unlike what all of humankind will go through on the path to flourishing.

The product of all of this is the book you now hold. We hope it helps you, your teams, your organization, and your world flourish. If you have a moment, send us an e-mail at info@enterpriseflourishing. com and let us know what impact this book has had in your life. We would love to hear from you. And if you would like more information about how The Flourishing Enterprise Collaborative might help you implement these ideas in your organization, let us know that as well. In the meantime, feel free to visit our collaborative's website at http://www.enterpriseflourishing.com or the Fowler Center's website at http://weatherhead.case.edu/centers/fowler for more information on this work. Here's to your flourishing!

Acknowledgements

We all stand on the shoulders of others in our life's work. Many generous people have directly impacted our collective effort on this particular project. We begin by gratefully acknowledging that this book would never have come into existence without the extraordinary vision of Char and Chuck Fowler. That vision motivated them to endow the Fowler Center for Sustainable Value in the Weatherhead School of Management at Case Western Reserve University, under whose aegis this book was written.

We are grateful for the inspired thinking and support of the members of the Fowler Center's Advisory Board: Jacqueline Cambata, J. Lyell Clarke III, David Cooperrider, Charles D. Fowler, Ronald E. Fry, Michele Hunt, Marcella Kanfer Rolnick, Jane Nelson, Peter Senge, and Nadya Zhexembayeva. Together they played an active role in shepherding our project in ways more typical of an executive leadership team than an advisory body.

This book is the culmination of hundreds of conversations and thousands of interactions that helped shape our research and provide incisive glimpses into the future of flourishing enterprise. The process started as a search for answers to new questions raised as we were insistently probed by our students, clients, colleagues, and friends. We are deeply grateful to all who offered gentle, and sometimes not so gentle, prodding along the way. We would especially like to mention Salima Adelstein, Dianne Anderson, Margaret Benefiel, Richard Boyatzis, Johanna Brickman Rebecca Chopp, Fred Collopy, Jude Currivan, Beau Daane, Andre Delbecq, Dan Duggan, Patsy Feeman, Sheron Fruehauf, Louis W. (Jody) Fry, Ron Fry, John Gardner, John Grim, Ibrahim Jaffe, Stuart L. Hart, James Keeley, John Laird, Jo Mackness, Carolyn Maraist, Judi Neal, Mohan Reddy, Miriam Sontz, James A. F. (Jim) Stoner, Bruce Svela, Mary Evelyn Tucker, Robert Widing, and Jackie Woodard.

Insights, ideas, and encouragement flowed freely from the business executives and thought leaders who gave of their time in interviews and conversations, which formed the basis for many of the findings that shaped our work. In particular, we wish to acknowledge the following people:

Jeffrey Abramson, Chairman and CEO of The Tower Companies

David Baker, Senior Manager of The Boeing Company

Jean Blackwell, CEO of the Cummins Foundation and Executive Vice President of Corporate Responsibility at Cummins Engine Company

Mark Brodeur, Global Sustainability Director for Purina.

Barrett C. Brown, President of MetaIntegral Academy, Principal at MetaIntegral Associates, and executive director of the Integral Sustainability Center at MetaIntegral Foundation

Mark Buckley, Vice President of Environmental Affairs at Staples

Marcelo Cardoso, Senior Vice President of Organizational Development and Sustainability at Natura

Jon Coleman, Director of Marketing and Sales at Ford Motor Company

Tom Curren, founder and President of Hawthorne Consultants

Jack Duan, founder and CEO of Gliding Eagle Inc.

John Duby, owner and founder of Serbaco, Inc.

Anders Ferguson, founding partner and leader of strategic marketing and business development at Veris Wealth Partners

Martin Goebel, founding principal of Moebius Partners LLC and founder of Sustainable Northwest

Seth Goldman, President and TeaEO of HonestTea

Marc Gunther, *Fortune* reporter and author

Jim Hamilton, former Vice President of Sustainability and External Affairs at Omya

Nick Hamon, CEO of Innovative Vector Control Consortium

Davida Herzl, cofounder and CEO at Aclima Inc.

Roland Herzl, Chairman of the Board for Aclima Inc.

Terry Herzl, board member for Aclima Inc.

Elliot Hoffman, cofounder of Just Desserts and True Market Solutions

Jeffrey Hollander, cofounder and former CEO of Seventh Generation

Ricardo Levy, cofounder of Catalytica and author of *Letters to a Young Entrepreneur*

Laura McKinney, former CEO of Galois

Ram Nidumolu, founder and CEO of InnovaStrat, Inc. and author of *Two Birds in a Tree: Timeless Indian Wisdom for Business Leaders*

Srikanth Padmanabhan, Vice President and General Manager of Cummins Emission Solutions

Rick Ridgeway, Vice President of Environmental Initiatives and Special Media Projects at Patagonia

Jonathan F. P. Rose, President of the Jonathan Rose Companies

Martin Rutte, President of Livelihood and coauthor of *Chicken Soup for the Soul at Work*

Carol Sanford, author of *The Responsible Business*

Amy Spatrisano, CMP, principal of MeetGreen and cofounder of the Green Meeting Industry Council

Françoise Trapenard, President of Telefonica Foundation

Skip Vaccarello, principal consultant with Korora Partners

Doug Verigan, Market Decisions

Kory Ward-Cook, CEO of the National Certification Commission for Acupuncture and Oriental Medicine

Cindy Wigglesworth, founder of Deep Change and author of *SQ21: The Twenty-One Skills of Spiritual Intelligence*

Nancy Wilson-Zavada, CMP, principal of Meetgreen and cofounder of the Green Meeting Industry Council

Steve Young, Senior Vice President of Marketing Communications at Eastern Bank

Years of opportunity to develop and test new material in the company of—and often in collaboration with—experienced managers and skeptical practitioners has been immensely helpful. We are indebted to the Weatherhead School of Management at Case Western Reserve University and to the Peter F. Drucker and Masatoshi Ito Graduate School of Management at Claremont Graduate University for allowing us to incorporate many of the new ideas and practices into their MBA and Executive Education programs.

We were gifted with an editor who recognized the power of flourishing enterprise even as it was just beginning to emerge as a book idea. Our gratitude goes to Margo Beth Fleming at Stanford University Press for her steadfast belief in our project and her extraordinary support during the year that our manuscript spent in her hands. In the process she became much more than a book editor; she was our writing partner, coach, friend, and staunch supporter, but also a wise critic who demanded excellence so that the final product would live up to its full potential. Margo and her colleague James Holt brought out the very best in our book. We also thank Stanford University Press's external reviewers, Vijay Sathe and Joel Makower, for the care and insight they provided.

Finally, we thank our families and closest friends, who provided the deep sense of connection and deep relationships that this book is all about. Lakshmi, Jenna, Ishana, Carita, Ervin, Alexander, David, Meg, Ruth, Jonathan, Lisa, Charlotte, Alex, Duncan, Mary Lou, Anna, and Jenell, we could not have done it without you.

About the Authors

Chris Laszlo, PhD, is associate professor of organizational behavior at Case Western Reserve University's Weatherhead School of Management, where he is also faculty research director at the Fowler Center for Sustainable Value. In addition, he is visiting associate professor at the Drucker School of Management and author of numerous books on sustainable business.

Judy Sorum Brown, PhD, is a poet and leadership educator. She is author of *A Leader's Guide to Reflective Practice* and *The Art and Spirit of Leadership*. Her work revolves around themes of leadership, change, renewal, learning, reflection, dialogue, and creativity. She has served as a White House Fellow and as vice president of the Aspen Institute.

John R. Ehrenfeld, ScD, is an educator and author of *Sustainability by Design* and (with Andrew Hoffman) *Flourishing: A Frank Conversation About Sustainability*. He is former director of the MIT Program on Technology, Business, and Environment. His continuing research focus is on sustainability and culture change.

Mary Gorham, MBA, CPCC, is a certified professional coach who helps leaders, teams, and organizations to flourish through executive coaching, leadership development, and organizational consulting. Her work empowers leaders in corporations, nonprofits, and higher education to make personal and organizational changes that build on their purpose, values, and vision.

Ilma Barros Pose, PhD, is a sustainability scholar and practitioner of Appreciative Inquiry, a Distinguished Fellow of the Fowler Center for Sustainable Value at Case Western Reserve University's Weatherhead School of Management, and an ELIAS (Emerging Leaders for Innovation Across Systems) fellow and member of the Presencing Institute.

Linda Robson is a sustainability scholar and practitioner. She is an advisor to the Fowler Center for Sustainable Value at Case Western Reserve University's Weatherhead School of Management, where she is a doctoral candidate in organizational behavior. She founded the university's campus sustainability program and served as its first sustainability coordinator.

Roger Saillant, PhD, is executive director of the Fowler Center for Sustainable Value at Case Western Reserve University's Weatherhead School of Management.

His extensive corporate experience includes seven years as CEO of Plug Power, and prior to that he served as a senior executive at Ford Motor Company.

Dave Sherman, DM, is a strategy, sustainability and social entrepreneurship advisor and researcher. He is president of Dave Sherman & Co. and cofounder of The Energy Collaborative. He helps executives formulate and execute break-through strategies that combine stakeholder-based insights with industry- and company-specific sources of advantage.

Paul Werder founded LionHeart Consulting, Inc. in 1983. He is also a spiritual teacher at the University of Spiritual Healing and Sufism. He has an extensive track record of weaving spiritual principles and practices into his work with leaders who are looking for genuine business success without the usual undesirable side effects.

Notes

Foreword

1. George Bernard Shaw, *Man and Superman* (New York: Penguin Classics, 2001).

Chapter 1

1. http://positivehandprints.org/what-is-a-positive-handprint, last accessed September 22, 2012.

2. Cited in John. Mackey and Raj Sisodia, *Conscious Capitalism: Liberating the Heroic Spirit of Business* (Boston: Harvard University Press, 2013), 137.

3. "Out of India," *The Economist,* March 3, 2011, http://www.economist.com/node/18285497, last accessed April 26, 2013.

4. "Want to Help Developing Countries? Sell Them Good Stuff—Cheap," *Wired,* September 27, 2010, http://www.wired.com/magazine/2010/09/st_essay_pennies, last accessed August 22, 2013.

5. "The World's Most Innovative Companies," *Forbes,* 2011, http://www.forbes.com/special-features/innovative-companies.html, last accessed April 26, 2013.

6. Cited in Luciana Hashiba, "Innovation in Well-Being—the Creation of Sustainable Value at Natura," Management Innovation Exchange, May 18, 2012, http://www.managementexchange.com/story/innovation-in-well-being, last accessed May 3, 2013.

7. M.I.T. *Sloan Management Review*/Boston Consulting Group (2011) survey, downloadable at http://sloanreview.mit.edu/feature/sustainability-strategy, last accessed September 22, 2012.

8. Sheila Bonini and Stephan Görner, "The Business of Sustainability: McKinsey Global Survey Results," October 2011, http://www.mckinsey.com/insights/energy_resources_materials/the_business_of_sustainability_mckinsey_global_survey_results.

9. In an interview, William Simon, head of Walmart USA, said, "A lot of things have distracted us from our pricing mission. . . . Sustainability and some of these other initiatives can be distracting if they don't add to every day low cost." Miguel Bustillo, "With Sales Flabby, Wal-Mart Turns to Its Core," *Wall Street Journal,* March 21, 2011, http://online.wsj.com/article/SB10001424052748703328404576207161692001774.html, last accessed April 24, 2013.

10. Ibid.

11. United Nations, *Millennium Development Goals Report 2011*,http://www.un.org/millenniumgoals/pdf/%282011_E%29%20MDG%20Report%202011_Book%20LR.pdf, last accessed July 28, 2012.

12. FAO, "100 Food Facts 2012: *100 Days to Rio +20, 100 Facts: Making the Link Between People, Food and the Environment,* http://www.fao.org/climatechange/31777-09a83cdc194ce209a6690bc8579f14bc8.pdf, last accessed April 23, 2013.

13. For trends in atmospheric carbon dioxide, see http://www.esrl.noaa.gov/gmd/ccgg/trends, last accessed March 24, 2014.

14. Justin Gillis, "Heat Trapping Gas Passes Milestone, Raising Fears," *New York Times,* May 10, 2013, http://www.nytimes.com/2013/05/11/science/earth/carbon-dioxide-level-passes-long-feared-milestone.html?pagewanted=all&_r=0, last accessed May 29, 2013.

15. "Climate Change: Evidence and Causes. A Report of the Royal Society and the US National Academy of Sciences," http://dels.nas.edu/resources/static-assets/exec-office-other/climate-change-full.pdf, last accessed March 24, 2014.

16. See Globescan, "Down to Business: Leading at Rio+20 and Beyond," *The Regeneration Roadmap,* a report of 1,600 sustainability experts at RIO + 20, June 15, 2012, http://www.globescan.com/component/edocman/?view=document&id=7&Itemid=591, last accessed September 23, 2012.

17. Well-known sustainability thought leaders who have adopted the term *flourishing* in preference to the word *sustainability,* or in order to give it greater meaning, include John Ehrenfeld, Andrew Hoffman, and Stuart Hart.

18. http://www.collinsdictionary.com/dictionary/english/flourishing, last accessed March 24, 2014.

19. http://www.oxforddictionaries.com/definition/english/flourish, last accessed March 24, 2014.

20. See Robert Bly, *Morning Poems* (New York: HarperCollins, 2007).

21. Cited in Mackey and Sisodia, *Conscious Capitalism,*. 88.

22. John R. Ehrenfeld, *Sustainability by Design: A Subversive Strategy for Transforming Our Consumer Culture* (New Haven, CT: Yale University Press, 2008).

23. Paul Hawken, *Blessed Unrest: How the Largest Social Movement in History Is Restoring Grace, Justice, and Beauty to the World,* reprint edition (New York: Penguin Books, 2008).

24. Danah Zohar and Ian Marshall, *Spiritual Intelligence: The Ultimate Intelligence* (London: Bloomsbury, 2001), 18.

25. Louis W. Fry and Cindy Graves Wigglesworth, "Toward a Theory of Spiritual Intelligence and Spiritual Leadership Development," paper presented at the Academy of Management, Montreal, Canada, 2010, 20.

26. Ian I. Mitroff and Elizabeth A. Denton, "A Study of Spirituality in the Workplace," *MIT Sloan Management Review,* July 15, 1999, http://sloanreview.mit.edu/article/a-study-of-spirituality-in-the-workplace, last accessed April 23, 2013.

27. Ibid.

28. Dalai Lama, *Ethics for the New Millennium* (New York: Riverhead Books, 1999), 22.

29. Beth Gardiner, "Business Skills and Buddhist Mindfulness," *Wall Street*

Journal, April 3, 2012, http://online.wsj.com/news/articles/SB1000142405270230 3816504577305820565167202, last accessed April 23, 2013. The professor referenced in the article is Jeremy Hunter, Drucker School of Management, Claremont Graduate University.

30. Robert A. Giacalone and Carole L. Jurkiewicz, *Handbook of Workplace Spirituality and Organizational Performance* (Armonk, NY: M.E. Sharpe, 2010).

31. Donde P. Ashmos and Dennis Duchon, "Spirituality at Work: A Conceptualization and Measure," *Journal of Management Inquiry* 9, no. 2 (2000): 134–145.

32. John Moyne and Coleman Barks, *Open Secret: Versions of Rumi,* ©1984 by John Boyne and Coleman Barks, reprinted by arrangement with the Permissions Company, Inc., on behalf of Shambhala Publications Inc., Boston, MA, http://www.shambhala.com.

33. Jeremy Lent, "Transcendence or Immanence? You Can Choose One, but Not Both . . . , *Finding the Li,* http://liology.com/?s=immanence, last accessed June 2, 2012; and Huston Smith, *Beyond the Postmodern Mind: The Place of Meaning in a Global Civilization* (Wheaton, IL: Quest Books, 2003).

34. Ibid.

35. From *The Selected Poems of Wendell Berry,* copyright © 1998 by Wendell Berry, used by permission of Counterpoint Press.

36. Ervin Laszlo, *The Self-Actualizing Cosmos: The Akasha Revolution in Science and Human Consciousness* (Rochester, VT: Inner Traditions, 2014).

37. We were troubled by the possibility of becoming ensnared in a contentious and potentially distracting debate between the two orientations, and it seems to us that framing the source of one's sense of connectedness in oppositional terms sets up a false choice ironically at odds with the sense of oneness and connectedness that drives our curiosity as a group of explorers—hence our inclusion of both immanence and transcendence.

38. "What Is Servant Leadership?" https://www.greenleaf.org/what-is -servant -leadership, last accessed April 25, 2013.

39. Judy Brown, *Simple Gifts* (Bloomington, IN: Trafford, 2011), 289.

40. Howard Behar with Janet Goldstein, *It's Not About the Coffee: Leadership Principles from a Life at Starbucks* (New York: Portfolio, 2013). Cited in Mackey and Sisodia, *Conscious Capitalism.*

Chapter 2

1. Denise Levertov, *Candles in Babylon* (New York: New Directions, 1982).

2. Patricia Aburdene, *Megatrends 2010: The Rise of Conscious Capitalism* (Newburyport, MA: Hampton Roads, 2007).

3. Louis W. Fry, "Toward a Theory of Spiritual Intelligence and Spiritual Leadership Development," Paper presented at the Academy of Management, Montreal, Canada, 2010.

4. Ian I. Mitroff and Elizabeth A. Denton, "A Study of Spirituality in the

Workplace," *MIT Sloan Management Review,* July 15, 1999, http://sloanreview.mit .edu/article/a-study-of-spirituality-in-the-workplace, last accessed April 23, 2013.

5. Louis W. Fry, *Toward a Theory of Spiritual Leadership,* Leadership Quarterly 14, no. 6 (2003): 693–727.

6. David W. Miller, *God at Work: The History and Promise of the Faith at Work Movement* (New York: Oxford University Press, 2007).

7. Heinz Köhler, *Intermediate Microeconomics: Theory and Applications* (Boston: Scott, Foresman, 1982).

8. Michael Porter, *Competitive Strategy: Techniques for Analyzing Industries and Competitors* (New York: Free Press).

9. Edith Penrose, *The Theory of the Growth of the Firm* (New York: Oxford University Press, 1959).

10. David J. Teece, Gary Pisano, and Amy Shuen, "Dynamic Capabilities and Strategic Management," *Strategic Management Journal* 18, no. 7 (1997): 509–533.

11. R. Edward Freeman, *Strategic Management: A Stakeholder Approach* (Cambridge, UK: Cambridge University Press, 1984).

12. Thomas G. Cummings and Christopher G. Worley, *Organization Development and Change,* 9th ed., (Independence, KY: Cengage, 2009).

13. T. F. Yaeger and P. F. Sorensen, "The Heritage, the Future, and the Role of Values in the Field of Organization Development, *Revue Sciences de Gestion* 65 (2008): 119–137.

14. Abraham Maslow, "A Theory of Human Motivation," *Psychological Review* 50, no. 4 (1943): 370; and *Religions, Values, and Peak-Experiences* (New York: Penguin, 1976).

15. Martin E. P. Seligman, *Authentic Happiness: Using the New Positive Psychology to Realize Your Potential for Lasting Fulfillment* (New York: Free Press, 2002); and *Flourish: A Visionary New Understanding of Happiness and Well-Being* (New York: Free Press, 2011).

16. Daniel Goleman, Richard Boyatzis, and Annie McKee, *Primal Leadership: Realizing the Power of Emotional Intelligence* (Watertown, MA: Harvard Business Review Press, 2002); Richard Boyatzis and Annie McKee, *Resonant Leadership: Renewing Yourself and Connecting with Others Through Mindfulness, Hope, and Compassion* (Watertown, MA: Harvard Business Review Press, 2005).

17. Margaret C. McKee, Jean H. Mills, and Cathy Driscoll, "Making Sense of Workplace Spirituality: Towards a New Methodology" *Journal of Management, Spirituality & Religion* 5, no. 2 (2008): 190–210.

18. Cliff Oswick, "Burgeoning Workplace Spirituality? A Textual Analysis of Momentum and Directions," *Journal of Management, Spirituality & Religion* 6, no. 1 (2009): 15–25.

19. For example, Louis W. Fry and Jon W. Slocum Jr., "Maximizing the Triple Bottom Line Through Spiritual Leadership," *Organizational Dynamics* 37, no. 1 (2008): 86–96.

20. Quoted in Michael Astor, "UN Discusses Creation of Gross National

Happiness," http://news.yahoo.com/un-discusses-creation-gross-national-happi
ness-003615190.html.

21. Chris Laszlo and Nadya Zhexembayeva, *Embedded Sustainability: The Next Big Competitive Advantage* (Stanford, CA: Stanford University Press, 2011).

22. *Greening* is defined here as an adoption of or alignment with the ideals or practices of the Green movement—for example, the greening of the mayor's platform.

23. World Economic Forum, *Global Risks 2011* Cologny/Geneva: WEF, 2011), 60.

24. Lynn S. Paine, *Value Shift: Why Companies Must Merge Social and Financial Imperatives to Achieve Superior Performance* (New York: McGraw-Hill, 2002); see also Thomas L. Friedman and Michael Mandelbaum, *That Used to Be Us: How America Fell Behind in the World It Invented and How We Can Come Back* (New York: Picador, 2012).

25. Business leaders across the globe are bringing spiritual practices into their management practices, including Jochen Zeitz at Puma (France), K. V. Kamath at Infosys (India), Marcelo Cardoso at Natura (Brazil), and Kazuo Inamori at Kyocera (Japan).

26. Jude Currivan, *HOPE: Healing Our People and Earth* (London: Hay House UK, 2011).

27. Don Beck and Christopher Cowan, *Spiral Dynamics: Mastering Values, Leadership, and Change : Exploring the New Science of Memetics* (Oxford, UK: Blackwell, 1996).

28. Friedman and Mandelbaum, *That Used to Be Us.*

Chapter 3

1. Malcolm Gladwell, *The Tipping Point: How Little Things Can Make a Big Difference* (New York: Back Bay Books, 2002).

2. Gladwell, without using the term *meme,* points us toward the notion that fast, permanent change is possible, an idea that first appeared in Richard Dawkins's book *The Selfish Gene.* The concept of the tipping point provides understanding about how such change occurs, as ideas and practices spread, sometimes like wildfire. Dawkins defined *meme* as an idea that is passed on from one human generation to another. It is the cultural equivalent of a gene, the basic element of biological inheritance. Humans, says Dawkins, can pass their ideas from one generation to the next, allowing the ideas to surmount challenges more flexibly and more quickly than the longer process of genetic adaptation and selection. Memes can be transmitted from one mind to another through writing, speech, gestures, rituals, or other imitable phenomena. And change can occur because a meme, or pattern of thought, begins to catch hold. Roger Saillant suggests that if we think of a meme as a self-replicating unit, we can see how, in the presence of healthy individuals, the idea replicates to other individuals, then to corporate cultures, which are replicated in other companies, then on to communities and eventually to the world. That is how flourishing, as a definition of health at all scales, can link individual flourishing to global flourishing for all systems for all times.

3. Charles S. Pierce, "How to Make Our Ideas Clear," *Popular Science Monthly* 12 (1878): 286–302, http://www.peirce.org/writings/p119.html, last accessed March 17, 2014.

4. Peter Senge, *The Fifth Discipline: The Art and Practice of the Learning Organization* (New York: Doubleday, 1990), 8

5. Thomas S. Kuhn, *The Structure of Scientific Revolutions,* 3rd. ed. (Chicago: University of Chicago Press, 1996).

6. Robert Bly, *Morning Poems* (New York: Harper Collins, 1998), 85.

7. John Ehrenfeld, *Sustainability by Design: A Subversive Strategy for Transforming Our Consumer Culture* (New Haven, CT: Yale University Press, 2008), 24.

8. Peter Senge, C. Otto Scharmer, Joseph Jaworski, and Betty Sue Flowers, *Presence: An Exploration of Profound Change in People, Organizations, and Society* (New York: Crown Business, 2005).

9. Otto Scharmer, *Theory U: Leading from the Future as It Emerges* (San Francisco: Berrett-Koehler, 2009).

10. Also characterized as *Homo Economicus.* See http://www.investopedia.com/terms/h/homoeconomicus.asp#axzz2CCkqNWAQ.

11. Erich Fromm, *To Have or to Be* (New York: Harper & Row, 1976).

12. Don Mayer, "Institutionalizing Overconsumption," in *The Business of Consumption: Environmental Ethics and the Global Economy* ed. Laura Westra and Patricia Werhane (Lanham, MD: Rowman & Littlefield, 1998) 67–90.

13. Paul Zane Pilzer, *God Wants You to Be Rich* (New York: Fireside, 1995).

14. For an excellent discussion of deeply embedded beliefs and assumptions, and how we might recognize, experiment with, and ultimately change them, see Robert Kegan and Lahey Laskow, *Immunity to Change: How to Overcome It and Unlock the Potential in Yourself and Your Organization* (Boston: Harvard University Press, 2009).

15. Melissa Korn, "Employed, but Not Engaged on the Job," *Wall Street Journal,* June 11, 2013, http://online.wsj.com/article/SB10001424127887323495604578539712058327862.html, last accessed June 14, 2013.

16. Chris Laszlo, *Sustainable Value: How Leading Companies Are Doing Well by Doing Good* (Stanford, CA: Stanford University Press, 2008).

17. This section is based on a working paper by Dave Sherman, "Cooperative Advantage: The Science and Art of Value Creation in the 21st Century," August 16, 2012.

18. The Greeks thought a tree was a tree because it contained an essence of "treeness." Social constructionists argue that a tree is what it is because we name it in the course of interacting with it.

19. Nora Bateson, *An Ecology of Mind: A Daughter's Portrait of Gregory Bateson,* video, 2012, http://www.anecologyofmind.com.

20. Ervin Laszlo, *The Self-Actualizing Cosmos: The Akasha Revolution in Science and Human Consciousness.* Rochester, VT: Inner Traditions, 2014. Much

of the material on the new sciences is from the work of this author in a dozen different books on the topic over three decades.

21. The argument here is that the evolution of species cannot be explained by Darwin's theory, in which chance mutations lead to the kind of finely balanced complexity we observe today. According to mathematical physicist Sir Fred Hoyle, the probability of a viable species emerging from random mutations in the genome is about the same as that of a hurricane blowing through a scrapyard and assembling a working airplane. This view becomes even more compelling in light of Harvard biologist Stephen Jay Gould's work on "punctuated equilibrium," which shows that new species evolve much faster than previously thought.

22. Cited in Ehrenfeld, *Sustainability by Design*.

23. For the work of Mary Evelyn Tucker and John Grim, see the Forum on Religion and Ecology at http://www.religionandecology.

24. Cited in Matthew T. Riley, "A Spiritual Democracy of All God's Creatures: Ecotheology and the Animals of Lynn White Jr.," in Stephen Moore, ed., *Divinanimality: Animal Theory, Creaturely Theology* (New York: Fordham University Press, 2014).

25. The Jewish mystical tradition of Kabbalah teaches that the Torah and the Bible are imbued with four levels of meaning: simple, homiletical, allegorical, and mystical. See Daniel C. Matt, *Zohar: Annotated and Explained* (Woodstock, VT: Skylight Paths, 2002).

26. William Shakespeare, *The Merchant of Venice*, Act V, scene i.

27. Swami Vivekanda, *Raja Yoga* (Calcutta: Advaita Ashrama, 1982), cited in Laszlo, *The Akasha Paradigm in Science*.

28. Kenneth J. Gergen, *Realities and Relationships: Soundings in Social Construction* (Cambridge, MA: Harvard University Press, 1994).

29. Humberto Maturana Romesin and Gerda Verden-Zöller, *The Origins of Humanness in the Biology of Love*. (Charlottesville, VA: Imprint Academic, 2008).

30. Humberto Maturana and Francisco Varela, "Machines and Living Things," in *Autopoiese to do Organização Vivo* (Porto Alegre: Medical Arts, 1997), 3.

31. Martin Heidegger, *Being and Time* (New York: Harper & Row, 2008). Originally English translation published 1962.

32. Eileen Luders, Florian Kurth, Emeran A. Mayer, Arthur W. Toga, Katherine L. Narr, and Christian Gaser, "The Unique Brain Anatomy of Meditation Practitioners: Alterations in Cortical Gyrification," *Frontiers in Human Neuroscience*, February 29, 2012, http://www.frontiersin.org/Human_Neuroscience/10.3389/fnhum.2012.00034/full. The authors speculate that "variations in insular complexity could affect the regulation of well-known distractions in the process of meditation, such as daydreaming, mind-wandering, and projections into past or future. Moreover, given that meditators are masters in introspection, awareness, and emotional control, increased insular gyrification may reflect an integration of autonomic, affective, and cognitive processes."

33. Cendri A. Hutcherson, Emma M. Seppala, and James J. Gross, "Loving-

Kindness Meditation Increases Social Connectedness," *Emotion* 8, no. 5 (2008): 720–724, http://spl.stanford.edu/pdfs/Hutcherson_08_2.pdf.

34. See, for example, the published work of James W. Pennebaker.

35. Stuart Hameroff, Roger Penrose, Henry P. Stapp, and Deepak Chopra, *Consciousness and the Universe: Quantum Physics, Evolution, Brain & Mind* (Cambridge, MA: Cosmology Science Publishers, 2011).

36. See Diane L. Coutu, "The Anxiety of Learning: An Interview with Edgar H. Schein," Harvard Business Review, March 2002, http://hbr.org/2002/03/the-anxiety-of-learning/ar/1, last accessed March 17, 2014.

37. Anthony Giddens, *The Constitution of Society: Outline of the Theory of Structuration* (Berkeley: University of California Press, 1984).

38. Stephen R. Barley, "Technology as an Occasion for Structuring: Evidence from Observations of CT Scanners and the Social Order of Radiology Departments," *Administrative Science Quarterly* 31 (1986): 78–108; Wanda J. Orlikowsky, "The Duality of Technology: Rethinking the Concept of Technology in Organizations," *Organizational Science* 3, no. 3 (1992): 398–427.

39. Richard Whittington, "Putting Giddens into Action: Social Systems and Managerial Agency," *Journal of Management Studies* 29, no. 6 (1992): 693–712.

40. For the purposes of analysis and design, Giddens divides the structure into four categories, but cautions that no such structure actually exists. It can be "found" only in the cognitive structure of the actors involved, or in the "memory traces" of the collective, in Giddens's words. The four categories are as follows:

1. Structure of signification: the rules by which the members of the organization make sense of the situation at any moment, in everyday language—in other words, their beliefs.

2. Structure of legitimation: the rules that give normative authority to the actions being taken, both in familiar routine activities and in confronting problematic situations.

3. Structure of domination: not domination in the sense of subjugation, but in the sense of potentiating action and empowering the actors. This structure is composed of two pieces:

   a. Allocative resources: the tools available to the actors to assist them in carrying out their normal routines.

   b. Authoritative resources: the ordering of actors who have power to actually allocate tools—again, in everyday terms, the power structure.

41. Daniel H. Kim, *Systems Archetypes I* (Cambridge, MA: Pegasus Communications, 1994), 26.

42. Chris Argyris and Donald Schon, *Organizational Learning: A Theory of Action Perspective* (Reading, MA: Addison-Wesley, 1978); Senge, *The Fifth Discipline*.

43. John Shook, *Managing to Learn: Using the A3 Management Process to Solve Problems, Gain Agreement, Mentor and Lead* (Cambridge, MA: Lean Enterprise Institute, 2008).

44. C. Otto Scharmer, *Theory U: Leading from the Future as It Emerges* (San Francisco: Berrett-Koehler, 2009); Senge, *The Fifth Discipline.*

45. Keith Hammonds, "Practical Radicals: Debra Meyerson," *Fast Company,* August 31, 2000, http://www.fastcompany.com/40529/practical-radicals.

Chapter 4

1. Roger Saillant and Jeremy Bendik-Keymer, "Sustainability Trajectory and Possibility," *International Journal of Ethical Leadership* 1 (2012): 81–85.

2. Eileen Luders, Florian Kurth, Emeran A. Mayer, Arthur W. Toga, Katherine L. Narr, and Christian Gaser, "The Unique Brain Anatomy of Meditation Practitioners: Alterations in Cortical Gyrification," *Frontiers in Human Neuroscience,* February 29, 2012, http://www.frontiersin.org/Human_Neuroscience/10.3389/fnhum.2012.00034/full.

3. See Mary Gorham, "21 Quick Tips to Get Present, Unleash Creativity, and Increase Your Effectiveness," 2013, http://www.MaryGorham.com/21-tips-offer - page, last accessed August 24, 2013.

4. Malcolm Gladwell, *Outliers: The Story of Success* (New York: Back Bay Books, 2011).

5. See, for example, Geoffrey Colvin, *Talent Is Overrated: What Really Separates World-Class Performers from Everybody Else* (New York: Portfolio, 2010).

Chapter 5

1. Parker Palmer, *A Hidden Wholeness: The Journey Toward an Undivided Life* (San Francisco: Jossey-Bass, 2009).

2. David Whyte, *River Flow: New & Selected Poems 1984–2007* (Langley, WA: Many Rivers Press, 2007).

3. Peter Senge, *The Fifth Discipline: The Art and Practice of the Learning Organization* (New York: Doubleday, 1990).

4. Aldo Leopold, *A Sand Country Almanac* (New York: Oxford University Press, 1949), 262.

5. Google, General Mills, Aetna, and Target are prominent examples of companies offering such meditation opportunities to employees.

6. See, for example, Todd Essig, "Google Teaches Employees To 'Search Inside Yourself,'" *Forbes,* April 30, 2012,http://www.forbes.com/sites/toddessig/2012/04/30/google-teaches-employees-to-search-inside-yourself.

7. Walter Isaacson, *Steve Jobs* (New York: Simon and Schuster, 2011).

8. Jon Kabat-Zinn, *Mindfulness for Beginners: Reclaiming the Present Moment—and Your Life* (Louisville, CO: Sounds True, 2011), http://www.soundstrue.com/shop/Mindfulness-for-Beginners/3793.pd.

9. In fact, in his *Forbes* article, Gelles highlights the work of Chade-Meng Tan, employee number 107 at Google, who in his book *Search Inside Yourself* (HarperOne 2012) declares that the benefits of meditation can be the catalyst for world peace. Daniel Goleman, author of *Emotional Intelligence: Why It Can*

Matter More Than IQ, writes in the foreword, "Meng was savvy in choosing his collaborators, like Zen teacher Norman Fischer, and Mirabi Bush, founding director of the Center for Contemplative Mind in Society, and Jon Kabat-Zinn, who pioneered the use of mindfulness in medical settings throughout the world. Meng knows quality." Meng also sought out and utilized Goleman's assistance in developing his mindfulness-based emotional intelligence curriculum at Google. His intention is to share it with anyone who could benefit, as "one of Google's gifts to the world."

10. Mihaly Csikszentmihalyi, *Flow: The Psychology of Optimal Experience* (New York: Harper Perennial, 2008).

11. Examples include the name of "The One" in the languages of the Jewish, Christian, and Islamic traditions. such as Elohim (Hebrew), Alaha (Aramaic), and Allah (Arabic). Other possibilities that have been effective for those with whom we have worked include Divine Light, Infinite Love, and Peace Within. The point is to find a name or word that is meaningful to you and that surfaces your sincere intention to uncover your direct connection to the spiritual mystery that can be experienced but not proven by conventional means.

12. Richard Boyatzis and Annie McKee, *Resonant Leadership: Renewing Yourself and Connecting with Others Through Mindfulness, Hope, and Compassion* (Watertown, MA: Harvard Business Review Press, 2005).

13. See, for example, the published work of James W. Pennebaker.

14. Julia Cameron, *The Artist's Way* (New York: Tarcher/Penguin, 2002).

15. See http://www.intensivejournal.org/about/aboutWorkbook.php, last accessed March 17, 2014.

16. Janine Benyus, *Biomimicry: Innovation Inspired by Nature* (New York, William Morrow, 2002).

17. Chris Hedges, *Empire of Illusion: The End of Literacy and the Triumph of Spectacle* (New York: Nation Books, 2009), 100.

18. See, for example, Rachel Kaplan and Stephen Kaplan, *The Experience of Nature: A Psychological Perspective* (New York: Cambridge University Press).

19. Frederick Franck, *The Zen of Seeing: Seeing/Drawing as Meditation* (New York: Vintage Books, 1973).

20. For more about the Center and its tools, see http://www.leadingeffectively.com/leadership-explorer.

21. William E. Henley, "Invictus," in *The Oxford Book of English Verse: 1250-1900,* ed. Arthur Quiller-Couch, (Bartleby.com, 1999), 1019.

22. John Coleman, "The Benefits of Poetry for Professionals," *HBR Blog,* November 27, 2012, http://blogs.hbr.org/2012/11/the-benefits-of-poetry-for-pro.

23. Sam Intrator and Megan Scribner, *Teaching with Fire* (San Francisco: Jossey-Bass 2003); Sam Intrator and Megan Scribner, *Leading from Within* (San Francisco, Jossey-Bass, 2007); Garrison Keiller, *Good Poems* (New York: Penguin, 2003).

24. For the past twenty years, Richard Boyatzis has been developing and refining a theory of intentional change utilizing longitudinal studies of competency development in order to understand leadership change and development (Boyatzis

and McKee, *Resonant Leadership*). Neurologists have discovered that the human brain is highly malleable and, contrary to previous belief, can continue to develop throughout adulthood. However, adult development can at times be extremely challenging. Meditation has been shown to foster adult development. The change process that Boyatzis calls *intentional change theory* has been shown through a number of longitudinal studies to foster directed development and personal transformation—straightforward yet quite powerful, and ideal for building skills and practicing ways of being that foster flourishing and sustainability.

25. Antonio Machado, *Border of a Dream* (Port Townsend, WA: Copper Canyon Press, 2013), English translation by Robert Bly, *Times Alone: Selected Poems of Antonio Machado* (Middletown, CT: Wesleyan University Press, 2011).

26. Daniel Goleman and Richard Boyatzis, "Social Intelligence and the Biology of Leadership," *Harvard Business Review,* September 2008, http://hbr.org/2008/09/social-intelligence-and-the-biology-of-leadership/ar/1.

27. Richard Boyatzis, Melvin Smith, and Nancy Blaize, "Developing Sustainable Leaders Through Coaching and Compassion," *Academy of Management Learning & Education,* 5, no. 1 (2006): 8–24.

28. Daniel Goleman, Richard Boyatzis, and Annie McKee, *Primal Leadership: Learning to Lead with Emotional Intelligence* (Watertown, MA: Harvard Business Review Press, 2004).

29. Boyatzis and McKee, *Resonant Leadership,* 44.

30. Ibid.

31. Tojo Thatchenkery and Carol Metzker, *Appreciative Intelligence: Seeing the Mighty Oak in the Acorn* (San Francisco: Berrett-Koehler, 2006).

Chapter 6

1. See http://www.centerforrightrelationship.com, last access March 17, 2014.

2. Paula Underwood, "Rule of Six," *Noetic Sciences Review,* Summer 1990, http://www.hartford-hwp.com/archives/41/129.html, last accessed March 17, 2014.

3. For more on the work of Liz Lerman, see the Liz Lerman Dance Exchange at http://www.danceexchange.org/toolbox. For the work of Arawana Hayashi, see http://www.arawanahayashi.com. For the work of Wendy Palmer, see http://www.consciousembodiment.com. All sites last accessed on March 17, 2014.

4. Frank J. Barrett, *Yes to the Mess: Surprising Leadership Lessons from Jazz* (Watertown, MA: Harvard Business Review Press, 2012).

5. Judy Brown, *A Leader's Guide to Reflective Practice.* (Bloomington, IN: Trafford, 2006).

6. http://www.valuescentre.com/products__services/?sec=cultural_values_assessment_%28cva%29, last accessed June 22, 2013. See also Richard Barrett, *The Values-Driven Organization: Unleashing Human Potential for Performance and Profit* (New York: Routledge, 2013).

7. Melissa Korn, "Employed, but Not Engaged on the Job," *Wall Street Journal,* June 11, 2013, http://online.wsj.com/article/SB10001424127887323495604578539712058327862.html, last accessed June 14, 2013.

8. To learn more about business as an agent of world benefit, see http://weather head.case.edu/centers/fowler, last accessed March 17, 2014.

Chapter 7

1. AI has already made significant contributions to organizational success because it enables change in a way that effectively compresses time and resources. The concept of W-Holistic AI purposefully adds to the AI experience of connection and wholeness. The W represents *wholeness* and directs our attention to the immanent need that stakeholders feel to experience a sense of connection at work; and AI is *holistic* because it perceives the individual as an autopoietic system— one that depends on its interaction with the larger system of which it is a part. Through reflective practices such as mindfulness, art and aesthetics, and nature immersion, W-Holistic AI creates additional opportunities for people to experience such wholeness and to feel a deep sense of connection to others and to the world around them, thus helping to generate system alignment that encourages individual and collective purpose to become more unified.

2. Peter Vaill, *Learning as a Way of Being: Strategies for Survival in a World of Permanent White Water* (San Francisco: Jossey Bass, 1996).

3. Marvin Weisbord, *Future Search: Getting the Whole System in the Room for Vision, Commitment, and Action* (San Francisco: Berrett-Koehler, 2010).

4. David Cooperrider, "Positive Image, Positive Action: The Affirmative Basis of Organizing," in *Appreciative Inquiry: An Emerging Direction for Organization Development,* ed. David Cooperrider Peter F. Sorensen Jr., Therese F. Yaeger, and Diana Whitney (Champaign IL: Stipes, 2001).

5. David Cooperrider, Peter F. Sorensen Jr., Therese F. Yaeger, and Diana Whitney, eds., *Appreciative Inquiry: An Emerging Direction for Organization Development* (Champaign IL: Stipes, 2001).

6. Shortly before his death, Peter Drucker spoke these words in an interview to David Cooperrider, who relayed them to the authors.

7. Vilsack, 2009. Comment made by Dave Sherman, who participated in the dairy industry's AI Summit.

8. See the Innovation Center for US Dairy at http://www.usdairy.com and the 2011 US Dairy Sustainability Report at http://www.usdairy.com/sustainability/Pages/Home.aspx.

9. At http://www.youtube.com/watch?v=jc_24Ya5Y4E.

10. Michael Ray, *The Highest Goal: The Secret That Sustains You in Every Moment* (San Francisco: Berrett-Koehler, 2004). The exercise is based on exploring a series of high-point moments when we were filled with amazing possibility for what our own life offered. These memories and the words we use to describe them become the clues we use to clarify what we are living for.

11. According to Hubbs and Brand (2005), "reflective journaling provides a vehicle that connects thoughts, feelings, and actions." For the purposes of W-Holistic AI, reflective journaling helps people connect to the inner realm, their thoughts

and feelings, and gives them the necessary time to connect that inner realm to what is surrounding them. Delaura L. Hubbs and Charles F. Brand, "The Paper Mirror: Understanding Reflective Journaling," *Journal of Experiential Education* 28, no. 1 (2005): 60–71.

Chapter 8
1. See for example, Robert A. Giacalone and Carole L. Jurkiewicz, *Handbook of Workplace Spirituality and Organizational Performance* (Armonk, NY: M.E. Sharpe, 2010).
2. Marge Piercy, *Circles on the Water* (New York: Knopf, 1982).
3. Mark Nepo, *Seven Thousand Ways to Listen* (New York: Free Press, 2012).

Afterword
1. Ram Nidumolu, C. K. Prahalad, and M. R. Ranagawami, "Why Sustainability Is Now the Key Driver of Innovation," *Harvard Business Review,* September 2009.
2. Raj Sisodia, David B. Wolfe, and Jag Sheth, J., *Firms of Endearment* (Saddle River, NJ: Prentice Hall, 2007).
3. Jim Collins, *Good to Great* (New York: HarperCollins, 2001).
4. James K. Harter, Frank L. Schmidt, and Corey L. M. Keyes, "Well-Being in the Workplace and Its Relationship to Business Outcomes: A Review: of the Gallup Studies," in Corey L. M. Keyes and Jonathan Haidt, *Flourishing: Positive Psychology and the Life Well Lived.* Washington, (DC: American Psychological Association, 2003).
5. David L. Cooperrider, Frank J. Barrett, and Suresh Srivastva, "Social Construction and Appreciative Inquiry: A Journey in Organizational Theory," in Dian Marie Hosking, H. Peter Dachler, and Kenneth J. Gergen (eds.), *Management and Organization: Relational Alternatives to Individualism* (Aldershot UK: Avebury, 1995).
6. Martin E. P. Seligman, Flourish: A Visionary New Understanding of Happiness and Well-Being (New York: Free Press, 2010).
7. Chade-Meng Tan, *Search Inside Yourself* (New York: HarperOne, 2012).
8. Peter Senge, *The Fifth Discipline: The Art and Practice of the Learning Organization* (New York: Doubleday Currency, 1990).
9. Karl Weick, *The Social Psychology of Organizing* (New York: Addison-Wesley, 1979).
10. Ibid, 87.
11. Martin E. P. Seligman and Mihaly Csikszentmihalyi, "Positive Psychology: An Introduction, *American Psychologist* 55 (200): 5–14.
12. Barbara Fredrickson, "The Value of Positive Emotions," *American Scientist* 91 (2003): 330–335.
13. Christopher Peterson and Martin E. P. Seligman, *Character Strengths and Virtues: A Handbook and Classification* (Washington, DC and New York: American Psychological Association and Oxford University Press, 2004).

14. David L. Cooperrider and Lindsey N. Godwin, "Positive Organization Development," in Kim S. Cameron and Gretchen M. Spreitzer (eds.), *The Oxford Handbook of Positive Organizational Scholarship* (Oxford, UK: Oxford University Press, 2011).

15. Martin E. P. Seligman, *Flourish: A Visionary New Understanding of Happiness and Well-Being* (New York: Free Press, 2010).

16. David L. Cooperrider, "The Concentration Effect of Strengths," *Organizational Dynamics* 42, no. 2 (2012): 21–32.

17. David Cooperrider and Ronald Fry, "Mirror Flourishing and the Positive Psychology of Sustainability," *Journal of Corporate Citizenship* 46 (2012): 3–12.

18. Stephen Post, *Why Good Things Happen to Good People* (New York: Random House, 2007).

19. Nicholas Christakis and James Fowler, Connected: The Surprising Power of Our Social Networks and How They Shape Our Lives—How Your Friends' Friends' Friends Affect Everything You Feel, Think, and Do (New York: Little, Brown, 2009).

20. Martin Buber, *I and Thou* (New York: Scribner's, 1958; translation originally published 1937).

21. David L. Cooperrider and Michelle McQuaid, "The Positive Arc of Systemic Strengths: How Appreciative Inquiry and Sustainable Designing Can Bring Out the Best in Human Systems." *Journal of Corporate Citizenship* 46 (2013).

22. Post, *Why Good Things Happen to Good People*.

23. Originally from Peter Vaill, *Managing as a Performing Art: New Ideas for a World of Chaotic Change* (San Francisco: Jossey-Bass, 1989).

Odyssey

1. Antoine de Saint-Exupéry, *The Wisdom of the Sands* (New York: Harcourt, Brace, 1950).

2. See also John R. Ehrenfeld and Andrew J. Hoffman, *Flourishing: A Frank Conversation About Sustainability* (Stanford, CA: Stanford University Press, 2013).

3. Michael Knecht, Chief Experience Officer, Loma Linda University Medical Center. Used with permission.

4. Soren Gordhamer, "Bill Ford on Compassion in Business, *Huffington Post*, February 28, 2010, http://www.huffingtonpost.com/soren-gordhamer/bill-ford-on -compassion-i_b_2781129.html, last accessed April 23, 2013.

5. Burt Helm, "Whole Foods' John Mackey Calls for a New Kind of "Conscious Capitalism," Inc.com, April 12, 2013, http://www.inc.com/burt-helm/john -mackey.html, last accessed April 23, 2013. See also John Mackey and Raj Sisodia, *Conscious Capitalism: Liberating the Heroic Spirit of Business* (Boston: Harvard University Press, 2013).

6. Quoted in Paul Kaihla, "Google Goes Spiritual," *Soul's Code*, http://www .soulscode.com/googles-stealth-launch-of-a-school-for-spirituality.

7. Chris Laszlo and Nadya Zhexembayeva, *Embedded Sustainability: The*

Next Big Competitive Advantage (Stanford, CA: Stanford University Press, 2011), Chapter 1.

8. Peter F. Drucker, *Landmarks of Tomorrow* (Piscataway, NJ: Transaction, 1996; originally published by Harper & Row, 1959).

9. Jeremy Hunter, "Is Mindfulness Good for Business?" *Mindful*, April 2013.

10. Ibid.

11. Knut Haanaes, Martin Reeves, Ingrid von Streng Velken, Michael Audretsch, David Kiron, and Nina Kruschwitz, "Sustainability Nears a Tipping Point," *MIT Sloan Management Review,* January 23, 2012, downloadable at http://sloanreview.mit.edu/feature/sustainability-strategy, last accessed September 22, 2012. See also the RIO+ 20 Report of 1,600 Sustainability experts at http://www.globescan.com/commentary-and-analysis/press-releases/press-releases-2012/207-down-to-business-leading-at-rio20-and-beyond.html, last accessed September 23, 2012.

12. Monastic Christians and reclusive spiritual men and women from other religious traditions who retreat from society cannot be said to influence world affairs in any direct-action terms. However, some would say that prayer and meditation can and do indirectly benefit others, for the faith-based and new science reasons alluded to in Chapter 3.

13. Howard Coward and Toby Foshay, eds., *Derrida and Negative Theology* (Albany: SUNY Press, 1992), 235–236.

Index

empowering women, 6, 7
energy efficiency, 164, 167
Engaged Buddhism, 80
enthusiasm, 101, 125, 174, 181
environmental ethics, 52
environmental impacts, 7, 36, 70, 71, 90–
    91, 98–99, 175, 183; environmental
    solutions initiatives, 124–25, 130–35;
    species extinction, 29–30
equitable societies, 6, 7
esthetic experience, 56
evolutionary biology, 17, 51, 203n21
executive pay and performance, 46, 47

Facebook, 182
Fairmount Minerals, 172, 177
faith, 211n11; beliefs based on, 50, 52–53,
    54; faith at work, 14, 16, 23; and
    meaning, 14, 54; vs. spirituality, 13–
    14, 16, 37, 72, 182
Fast Company, 66
fear, 33, 64, 69, 95–96
Federation of Industries of the State of São
    Paulo (FIESP), 141–49
financial crisis of 2008–2009, 36, 47
financial regulations, 24
Financial Times, 80
firms of endearment, 163
Fischer, Norman, 206n9
flourishing: mirror flourishing, 174–78;
    PERMA model of, 172, 173, 174,
    176; and prosperity, 9, 19, 28, 35, 43,
    58, 67, 155, 159, 167, 170, 178, 185–
    86; relationship to caring, 37, 67,
    164; relationship to connectedness,
    36, 39–40, 67, 97–98, 113–14, 151,
    153–54, 156, 159, 162, 164, 183,
    185–87, 189; relationship to leader-
    ship, 66, 97–103, 121–22, 127–28,
    162, 181, 183; relationship to reflec-
    tive practices, 19, 35, 37–38, 39–40,
    49, 55–67, 68, 73–74, 75–78, 82,
    84, 87, 88, 94–95, 96, 98, 99, 103,
    130, 139, 151–52, 155, 162, 170,
    178, 183, 186, 207n24; relationship
    to spirituality, 8, 13, 14, 15, 18–21,
    34, 55–58, 66, 73, 80, 120, 151, 155,
    162, 167–68, 179–86; sustainability
    as, 7–11, 19–20, 31–32, 35–36, 40,
    49, 57, 60, 65–67, 94, 104, 114, 129–
    30, 151, 159, 164–65, 166–70, 172–
    73, 176, 178, 179–80, 182, 183, 184,

198n17. See also global flourishing;
    individual flourishing; organizational
    flourishing; systems level flourishing;
    team flourishing
Flourishing Enterprise Collaborative,
    189–90
flow and mindfulness, 81–82
Flowers, Betty Sue: Presence, 40
focus, 73, 113, 181, 184; and expansion,
    69
food security, 5, 6
Forbes, 2, 205n9
Ford, Bill, 31, 181
Ford Motor Company, 13, 31, 181
Fortune, 119
Fortune Global 500, 46
Fowler Center for Sustainable Value, 179,
    190; Advisory Board, 154, 188
Francis of Assisi, 52
Franck, Frederick, 92
Frederickson, Barbara, 113, 128
Friedman, Thomas, 33
Frost, Robert: "The Road Not Taken", 95
Fry, Louis W.: on spirituality, 12, 22
Fry, Ron, 174
Fuller, Connie, 128
Future Search, 126, 139, 150

Galileo Galilei, 53–54
Gaser, Christian, 203n32
Gates, Bill, 73
Gekko, Gordon: on greed, 41
Gelles, David, 80, 205n9
General Electric, Ecomagination initia-
    tive, 125
General Foods, 94
General Mills, 80, 182, 184, 205n
General Motors, 24
geopolitical conflict, 29
Gerstner, Lou, 46
Giddens, Anthony: on organizational cul-
    ture, 63–64, 204n40
Gioia, Dana: Can Poetry Matter?, 94
Gladwell, Malcolm: Outliers, 73; Tipping
    Point, 38; on tipping points, 38, 165,
    201n2
global flourishing, 35, 44, 45, 63, 68, 69,
    70, 71, 74, 176; as 150-year project,
    10, 67, 77, 96, 122, 185, 189; rela-
    tionship to individual flourishing, 15,
    57–58, 174, 186–87, 189, 201n2; re-
    lationship to organizational flourish-

Meyerson, Debra: on tempered radicals, 66–67
microeconomics, 23
Millennium Development Goals (MDGs), 5, 141, 146
mindfulness, 56, 100, 101, 169, 206n9, 208n1; and flow, 81–82; mindfulness meditation, 55, 75, 78–81, 146–47, 181, 184, 186
mindsets, 12, 40, 49, 62, 65–66, 183
mirror flourishing, 174–78
MIT, 64–65
Mitroff, Ian: on spirituality, 12, 22–23
MIT Sloan Management Review, 3, 12
monetarism, 24
Moon, Richard, 108
motivation and spirituality, 8, 23, 32–34
music, 55, 72, 78, 81, 89, 116–17, 140; jazz improvisation, 108–12; singing, 95–96

Narr, Katherine L., 203n32
National Grid, 173
Native Americans, 89, 91–92, 107–8, 116
Natura, 2–3, 7, 10, 163, 182, 201n25
natural resources, 6, 7, 20, 41, 42, 43, 70, 71, 183
nature immersion, 36, 56, 62, 72, 75, 90–92, 140, 208n1
neoclassical economics, 23, 47
Nepo, Mark: "The Appointment", 156–57
net zero goal setting, 164
neuroscience, 26, 56–57, 72, 101, 167, 203n32, 206n24; mirror neuron system, 175
newsworthiness, 4
New York Times, 53–54, 94
Nidumolu, Ram, 161–62
Nike, 90
Novo Nordisk, 173

OAT, 167, 176
obliquity, 160–61, 166, 178
Oneida Nation, 89, 91, 107–8
oneness: naming "The One", 206n11; in nature, 53, 57; striving for, 16–17, 18, 33, 56–57, 143, 144
organizational culture, 4–5, 37–38, 59, 63–67, 161, 170, 201n2
organizational development (OD), 26
organizational flourishing, 35, 69, 84,

151, 152–53, 186; and organizational reflective practices, 8, 37–38, 57–67, 68, 104–22, 127, 128, 152; relationship to global flourishing, 57–58, 122, 168–69, 170, 179, 183, 185; relationship to individual flourishing, 15, 36, 43–45, 57–59, 65, 66, 73, 97–103, 104, 156, 168–69, 170, 172–73, 174, 176, 178; relationship to leadership, 66, 97–103, 121–22, 127–28, 162, 170, 180–82, 183
organizational identity, 161–62, 170
organizational inertia, 61
organizational learning, 25, 77, 155
Original Three Tenor's Concert, 116, 144
Outward Bound experiences, 91

Paine, Lynn S.: *Value Shift*, 32
Palmer, Wendy, 108
partner relationship, 13, 44, 47, 105–7, 161, 173, 187–88
Pascal, Blaise: on distractions, 55; *Pensées*, 55
Patrick, Deval, 173
Penrose, Edith: *The Theory of the Growth of the Firm*, 25
philanthropy, 28
Pierce, Charles S.: on belief, 38
Piercy, Marge, 155
Pigou, Arthur, 23–24
Plantronics, 182
Plato, 53
Plotinus, 53
poetry, 93–95, 138, 140, 156–57
Porter, Michael: *Competitive Advantage*, 46; on competitive strategy, 24, 46; *Competitive Strategy*, 46
positive psychology, 26, 128, 165, 171–72
Post, Stephen: on doing good-doing well dynamic, 175, 177–78; *Why Good Things Happen to Good People*, 177
Prahalad, C. K., 161
presencing, 91, 139, 150; Presencing Institute, 108; Scharmer on, 40, 125–26, 144
prices, 4–5, 47, 49, 197n9
PricewaterhouseCoopers, 171
process redesign, 124
profit, 5, 24, 41, 67, 103, 164; and obliquity, 160; relationship to dialogue, 113, 119; relationship to sustainability, 2, 3, 30–31, 32, 185

Milton Keynes UK
Ingram Content Group UK Ltd.
UKHW041815150224
437889UK00004B/63/J